WILLIAM
HOWARD
TAFT

CONFIDENT
PEACEMAKER

WILLIAM HOWARD TAFT

CONFIDENT PEACEMAKER

BY

DAVID H. BURTON

SAINT JOSEPH'S UNIVERSITY PRESS
PHILADELPHIA

AND

FORDHAM UNIVERSITY PRESS
NEW YORK

LIBRARY OF CONGRESS CATALOGING-IN-PUBLICATION DATA

Burton, David Henry, 1925-

   William Howard Taft : confident peacemaker / David H. Burton.

     p. cm.

   Includes bibliographical references and index.

   ISBN 0-916101-51-7 (cloth : alk. paper)

   ISBN 0-916101-50-9 (pbk. : alk. paper)

   1. Taft, William H. (William Howard), 1857-1930—Views on peace. 2. United States—Foreign relations—1865-1921. I. Title.

   E762.B869 2004

   973.91'2'092—dc22

                  2004012433

Co-published by:

SAINT JOSEPH'S UNIVERSITY PRESS
5600 City Avenue
Philadelphia, Pennsylvania 19131-1395
www.sju.edu/sjupress/

AND

FORDHAM UNIVERSITY PRESS
Bronx, New York 10458-5172
www.fordham.edu/fordhampress/

Members of the Association of Jesuit University Presses

IN MEMORIAM
Alec Campbell

OTHER BOOKS BY DAVID H. BURTON

American History - British Historians

An Anglo-American Plutarch

British-American Diplomacy 1895-1917

Cecil Spring Rice A Diplomat's Life

Clara Barton: In the Service Of Humanity

Edwin Arlington Robinson

Oliver Wendell Holmes, Jr.

Oliver Wendell Holmes, What Manner of Liberal

Political Ideas of Justice Holmes

Holmes-Sheehan Correspondence

Progressive Masks

The Learned Presidency

Theodore Roosevelt

Theodore Roosevelt: Confident Imperialist

Theodore Roosevelt and His English Correspondents

Theodore Roosevelt American Politician

William Howard Taft in the Public Service

Taft, Holmes and the 1920s Court

Taft, Wilson, and World Order

Taft, Roosevelt and the Limits of Friendship

Contents

Preface ix

Introduction xi

Ordered Beginnings 1

Learning Curve 27

Evolving Vision 59

World Order in the Offing 85

Conservative Internationalist 115

Bibliography 121

Appendices 125

    The Taft-Katsura Agreement (1905) 126

    The Havana Speech (1906) 128

    The Root-Takahira Agreement (1908) 135

    Canadian Reciprocity Treaty (1911) 137

    Arbitration Treaties (1911) 143

    Dollar Diplomacy (1912) 145

    The Warrant From History (1915) 149

    Self-Determination (1919) 150

    Senator Lodge on the League of Nations (1919) 153

    Criticism Should Be Constructive (1919) 157

    To Make Peace Secure (1919) 161

    The Victory Program (1918) 167

Index 169

PREFACE

This study is built upon both a synthesis and an interpretation of the foreign policy ideas and initiatives of William Howard Taft. It encompasses the whole of his public career as a statesman, from his years as civil governor of the Philippines through his tenure as chief justice of the Supreme Court. Consequently it draws on the well-regarded findings of historians of his diplomacy, both before and during his presidency, as well as his thoughts on international affairs during World War I. Even so, there are important aspects of his diplomacy that are not part of the inherited canon, particularly with regard to the role Taft played in the months immediately after war broke out in 1914. Among others, but in a manner second only to Woodrow Wilson, he was fully alive to the need to preserve the peace of the world through a new version of international organization. Therefore this book is an investigation and an interpretation of Taft's internationalism. He moved from his basic belief in the theory and practice of balance of power through the application of dollar diplomacy that played on the economic realities of geopolitics as determining elements in power politics. Then in response to the calamity of World War I, Taft came to a recognition that world peace, in the last analysis, must be based on a combination of idealism and realism, of high-minded principles placed and kept in effect by force deliberately chosen and carefully applied. In a word, Taft's international mind-set had evolved over the course of some twenty years. In the process he concluded that only through an international organization, be it a League of Nations or a League to Enforce Peace, could order in the world be maintained. In so saying he insisted that the United States must play an active, nay, a leadership role in the international affairs of the twentieth century. And so it was to be.

This is the time and place to acknowledge the support and encouragement given this undertaking. Carmen Croce has been a friend to the proposal in the first instance and ever faithful through its publication. David Contosta read the manuscript, providing me with fresh insights and an astute perspective on the work. Seth Taft took a great interest in this new view of Taft-Roosevelt in action, that is greatly valued. Dori Pappas once again demonstrated that she is an ideal twenty-first century amanuensis. Thank you one and all.

INTRODUCTION

By heritage and by training, by instinct and by temperament, William Howard Taft was a man of peace, peaceful in his intent and peaceful in his ways. By reason of his upbringing, exemplified by his father's public service, and because of his legal training, he was given to resolve issues that appealed to law and the forms of government that had issued forth. His persona and his character, that is, his outlook regarding the social contract, and a willingness to abide by a code of ethics rooted in religion and in reason, spell out fully the kind of public servant he was to become. What Taft sought to do, and indeed, insisted on doing, was to apply his perspective and his values in matters of politics at home and abroad.

To come to an awareness and an appreciation of Taft's conception and execution of world-ordered diplomacy, it is necessary to understand the man, *sans peur et sans reproche*, so that his diplomatic endeavors, in the name of peace not war, cannot but be viewed as natural to him and unquestionably sincere. However, diplomacy always assumes a context, and it was the changing history of his years of prominence and power affecting diplomacy, 1900 to 1920, that imparts an evolutionary strain to the diplomatic solutions he proposed. Early in his career he judged that balance of power was a way to preserve peace in the Far East. Fierce national rivalries giving rise to wars, and the Great War itself, changed all that. In consequence Taft, along with Woodrow Wilson, spoke out strongly for some kind of league among and between nations in order to make the world free.

This study of Taft as diplomat is an important part of a total account of his life and of his life and times. As Civil Governor in the Philippines and as Secretary of War, he was given important diplomatic responsibilities by Presidents McKinley and Roosevelt, and as president he gladly assumed them in the name of a more ordered and peaceful world.

Taft's diplomatic endeavors in search of peace during and after World War I round out his role as an international statesman, although he still sustained an interest in international law as chief justice. It becomes a matter of appreciating the efforts that go into a failed undertaking, whether it be the work of Taft or Woodrow Wilson, both of whom tried unsuccessfully to achieve the reverse image of American diplomacy in those years.

In William Howard Taft's calculus, law, order, and peace were the image of triangulated stars in the firmament of international relations. Each was essential to the other after the fashion of a Newtonian universe inhabited by nations. It required law and order to produce and maintain peace. Without law there could be no order; only in an ordered world could law operate effectively, while peace between nations was a presupposition of, and a result of, responsible behavior by nations toward one another.

Responsible behavior is exactly what Taft's diplomacy envisioned. The means whereby this order could be brought about assumed an evolutionary principle to be at work. It was not found in the simplistic mechanism of survival, but in a pragmatic approach that adjusted to a changing international environment. Change was inevitable but it must come about as a result of deliberate, enlightened decision-making, and not by the *Sturm und Drang* mentality that had come to dominate the Old World—survival of the fittest in its meanest sense. This evolutionary design, though not solely typical of Taft, was nonetheless readily identifiable in his diplomatic response to changing conditions in the Orient, the Americas, and finally in Europe. The avid student of William Graham Sumner's promotion of Social Darwinism had evolved into a pragmatist in affairs of state as this study of Taft's life in diplomacy bears out.[1]

A full understanding of William Howard Taft as a man of peace necessarily leads back to his early life before he entered public service.

His family, his upbringing where his private world was ordered and secure, are the beginnings. Education and legal training that followed nurtured his choice of community involvement as a lawyer, judge, and government attorney, and what appeared to him, his family, and his friends, to be destiny. Appointment as a federal appeals judge might or might not lead on to a seat on the Supreme Court. Attention must be given to each of these steps and the experiences that helped to give form and texture to an evolving pattern of principles applicable to diplomacy. It is less satisfying if his career is separated from his private life, shaped as it was by inherited and inbred values that he brought to his handling of foreign policy.

In order to project the image of Taft as diplomat more distinctly, twelve key documents are included in an Appendix. They add detail and depth to this study, further authenticating the seriousness of Taft's commitment to an ordered world.

NOTES

[1] The best analysis of the intellectual environment nurturing Taft and his generation remains Philip Wiener's *Evolution and the Founders of Pragmatism* (Cambridge: Harvard University Press, 1949).

1. ORDERED BEGINNINGS

The world of William Howard Taft's early years was serene and secure but not without some uncertainties. According to the times and the customs, men—and it was a male bastion society—had to make their own way to success, or at the very least out of poverty. Some succeeded and others did not, reflecting the anomalies of a free polity and free-swinging socio-economic system. Make no mistake about it, achievement was measured mostly by material gains, from shirt sleeves to frock coat, or to vulgarize the dictum of the work ethic with a supernatural touch, God loves a winner. Looked at from another angle, capitalism and the Constitution were conjoined, let them never to be torn asunder. This union tended to produce an optimism as well as a confidence in the rightness of things in a nation that was still emerging from the trauma of a long and bloody civil war.[1]

By the time Will Taft was ten (he was born in 1857) the triumph of the Union had pointed the nation in a new direction, confirming the future of constitutional government for the states and the nation, for the south and the west. Order had been restored, and there was a sense of a new beginning, a mood that would have a shaping effect on Taft's generation. Not yet recognized as a world power in the immediate post-war years, the nation would witness the purchase of Alaska in 1867, enlarging an American presence in the hemisphere. Dismissed by some critics as "Seward's folly," the purchase appeared to speak, almost unconsciously, to the inevitable extension of American power.[2]

In the 1870s and 1880s this extension confined itself to the western land frontier, looking to the completion of a continental empire. Subduing the obstacles encountered was greatly facilitated by the construction of continental railroads, the first of which, the Union Pacific, was in operation by 1869. Civil War veterans were joined by waves of immigrant labor to cultivate the Great Plains, mine the mineral lodes, and clear the land of timber. American agriculture became not merely self-sufficient but a soon-to-be supplier of food and other farm products to world markets. Between industry and agriculture the United States was poised to challenge and then surpass in economic strength older, long dominant nations. Such was the success at home before the century ended, that the lure of overseas markets became irresistible. It was in the 1890s that various forces at work within the nation combined to bring the United States onto the world stage. Added to industrial capacity, farm expansion (well into Taft's years as president, the majority of America's employed was tilling the soil), tending the herds, and exploiting the resources of iron, coal, oil, natural gas, and timber readily accounted for America's place in the sun. But there is more. The apparent success of elected governments at all levels added luster on the outside while within was the unyielding conviction that America was indeed, in Jefferson's phrase, "the world's last, best hope." Judgments varied as to why this was so. Divine Providence, Americans as God's new chosen people, was most often on the lips of preachers in pulpits and otherwise, and in the unspoken thoughts of millions of people. Among the ruling class, business tycoons, railroad magnates, and banking moguls, it was more usually a case of the strong survive and the weak perish, all according to the Natural Law. Andrew Carnegie, the steel king-pin, put it directly: competition is hard on the individual but it is best for the race that the strong survive. Other businessmen tried to carry water on both shoulders. Daniel Drew, the stock manipulator, has been epitomized as a "master fleecer of lambs and founder of Drew Theological Seminary." In like vein John Fiske in his highly regarded study, *Outlines of Cosmic Philosophy*, interpreted evolution as part of the divine plan. And so the arguments for American greatness had come full circle.[3]

How was the nation's strength to be measured? There were three criteria: economic productivity, political stability, and "the fighting edge." The fighting edge had been part of American myth and reality since earliest times. The conquest and settlement of one of the great continents came about by war (the Mexican War) and by diplomacy (Seward's folly), and by said means the future greatness of the nation would be assured. Given the geopolitical facts, what would be more vital to America's place in the sun than a great navy? In 1890 Alfred Thayer Mahan published *The Influence of Sea Power on History*. Scholarly though it was, it proved seminal in the development of navalism in the United States, and well into the lifetime of William Howard Taft the nation's naval power was rated equal with that of Great Britain. Yet for a country sitting astride the two great oceans of the world, navalism came naturally and was given greater appeal and purpose as the continental frontier began to close. Of great interest to Washington were the Hawaiian Islands where both merchants and missionaries had been plying their diverse trades for some decades. The coup of 1893 that sought the overthrow of the royal government (Hawaii was a kingdom) by American sugar planters was stifled by President Cleveland who was anti-expansionist. But in 1898 the Islands were annexed by the United States as it became a Pacific power with possession of the Philippines, one of the fruits of the Spanish American War. The American empire was aborning. There was no more forceful spokesman in the name of American expansion than Senator Albert Beveridge. To him dominion over lesser peoples was the right of a master race. Rebutting those who feared colonial possessions would foul the waters of republican rule, Beveridge trumpeted empire over isolation in taking up the white man's burden whether in the Hawaiian Islands or the Philippine Islands.[4] That empire would suddenly involve William Howard Taft who, to his own surprise and that of many others as well, became the first civil governor of the Philippines, an appointment launching his career in diplomacy.

Taft is a convincing example that statesmen are made, not born, that whatever qualities of mind and spirit are theirs they must, of necessity, have the opportunity to use these gifts in carrying through the art of diplomacy. He was, if anything, born to be a judge. Such was the nature of his inner self, to dispense justice through the administration of the law. And one day he would preside as chief justice of the United States Supreme Court, but not before he had promoted his ideas which, when reduced to their essence, sought to bring about peace through diplomacy. Despite the seeming difference between diplomat and jurist, in each of these guises he comes across as a disciple of order under law.

From his first years Taft was aware and appreciative of his family's history. Ordinarily identified as a good Ohio man, someone who always had his plate right side up when offices were being handed out, he was as much a New Englander as a Mid-Westerner. The first Taft, Robert by given name, arrived in Massachusetts Bay Colony about 1670. He was a "plain, unlettered man," a carpenter by trade. He settled permanently in Mendon, worked hard, and in the long run prospered. One of his descendents, Samuel, maintained a tavern where President Washington, on a tour of New England, stopped to sup. The story became part of family lore. But it remained for a later generation to bring the family notice in the person of Taft's father, Alphonso. Again the story would be told to successive generations how as a teenager he walked from Townshend, Vermont, his native village, to New Haven to enroll at Yale College, class of 1833. After graduating with honors he taught school for a while, studied law, and went West to grow up with the country. Cincinnati on the Ohio River suited him just fine, small enough for a newcomer to make his mark but large enough to cultivate intelligent, successful, and important people.

In the formation of the mind and spirit of William Howard Taft both his father and mother worked together to mould the boy into the man. In the process their contributions were different and distinct, but a meshing of talents and wills did much to shape what their son would

become. Alphonso Taft was simultaneously ambitious and self-effac-
ing. In some ways he would have been content to live out his life as a
Cincinnati judge; he was one of the leaders of the city's intellectual and
cultural endeavors. As a family the Tafts were never estimated to be
rich but rather to be educated and forward-looking. In describing his
ancestors William Howard's father summed up his own outlook: "men
who knew how to get rich and men who dared to be poor." The senior
Taft was politically active: he twice sought the Republican nomination
for governor and twice failed. He later served briefly in the Grant
administration as Secretary of War and Attorney General. President
Arthur named him American Minister to the Austro-Hungarian Empire
and again briefly as American Minister to Russia. Whatever he attempted by way of election or selection he did out of a felt need to serve his
country and his fellow citizens.[5]

Louise Torrey Taft, Alphonso's wife, was well-educated and widely
read. She had been a student at Mount Holyoke Academy and attended public lectures at Yale. She took her duties as wife and mother with
the utmost seriousness. Her second son, Will, the first child having died
in infancy, she acknowledged as her favorite among her children.
Though protective of him, she nonetheless pushed him forward in
school, and for that matter, in life. Taft responded positively to this
mothering. As a grown man and in public offices he often invited her
to accompany him on official trips. Such parenting encouraged him to
rely on his family when in need of advice and support. As a family the
Tafts came to prefer the Unitarian church, the least theological denom-
ination. If Unitarianism did not amount to free thinking about God and
man, it came close to that and was, therefore, out of step with mainstream Protestantism. When approached about assuming the presidency
of Yale in 1899 Taft put his beliefs plainly: "I am a Unitarian. I believe
in God. I do not believe in the divinity of Christ. And there are
many other parts of the orthodox creed to which I can not subscribe.

I am not, however, a scoffer at religion but on the contrary recognize, in the fullest manner, the elevating influence it has had and will always have in the history of mankind."[6] In so saying Taft was in step with many of the Founding Fathers whose religion was more personal than theological. Echoes of Ben Franklin . . . religion has its uses!

Partly by preference and partly by inculcation Will Taft led an ordered life, and order became, in consequence, part of his being. The Taft family, archtypically upper middle class at the time, helped to set standards for achievement and aspiration. Society was mobile but nonetheless structured to such a degree that the masses voted but the classes governed. The order in society was not rigid but it was real and the young Will Taft grew up in the belief that things were as they should be. It is hard to overstress the function of the family in his upbringing. His father insisted on accomplishment through hard work, his mother taught him the ways of compassion, father and mother standing together projected the image of a tightly knit family. Through his long and distinguished career he never made a major decision without consulting parents at first, later his brothers and once he married, his wife. He was to raise his own three children in the same loving, caring way. To Taft, nay to the Tafts for generations to come, the family was the all important social unit, at the base of the social pyramid. It was the source and the model of order, perhaps in the long run, showing the way to achieve an ordered world through diplomacy.

To trace the life of Taft from family circle, to schooling at Yale and in the study of law, to his first appointment as a local judge, then a superior court seat, and from there to Solicitor General of the United States in the Harrison administration, and as the century wound down, to a federal appeals court judge, the progress of his career appeared to be an ordered succession.

Yale was, in a real way, an extension of the family. Entering with the class of '78 he was quickly distinguished both by reason of academic achievement and reputation for honesty in all manner of ways common to college. Predictably he came under the influence of the college faculty. Henry A. Beers, an authority on romantic literature, instilled in him a lifelong fondness for the novels of George Eliot. This is important to note since years later, Taft was to recall the socio-economic doctrines expounded by William Graham Sumner, the antithesis of Beers in tone and timber. The fact is that Yale offered students the opportunity to have a varied but comprehensive education, and Taft's courses ranged from Livy and Horace to mechanics and physics. In light of his early intentions, not fully integrated until his last years at Yale, to seek a career in public affairs, one book that he studied, Woolsey's *Introduction to International Law*, proved to have a guiding effect. Along with the lectures and early writings of Sumner, these two Yale professors imparted to Taft the received wisdom (out of Woolsey) and contemporary scientific thought (by way of Sumner) that the future diplomat would respond to in the course of shaping his own public philosophy anent international politics.

It was a fortunate coincidence that at the very time Taft enrolled, Yale had made the move from a small, almost local college, to become a university in the true sense, that is, providing universal knowledge for all who seized the day. And freshman Will Taft was primed to do just that. He read DeTocqueville's *Democracy in America* and Schwegler's *History of Political and Social Sciences*. Horace Porter's *Human Intellect* and Fawcett's *Political Economy* were part of his senior year reading. In effect he had taken early steps away from a parochial orientation as his mind opened to the world around him. Unconsciously perhaps, but surely, Yale had encouraged him to meet the challenges: what does he know of America who only America knows. Having set forth this general proposition no account of the Yale experience would be complete without giving detailed attention to the influence of his professors, most prominent among them William Graham Sumner, and one tome in particular, Theodor Dwight Woolsey's *International Law*. They did not in fact complement one another, setting up competing systems for understanding the world of the day, and how it might be best governed.[7]

The Woolsey book was a scholarly primer that dealt with the history of international law and its contemporary practice. However theoretically it read in places, the student could not but come away from the book feeling that Woolsey had his feet on the ground. Early in his presentation he stated plainly "a law of nations can grow up only by the consent of the parties to it." The voluntary, in other words, must combine with the wisdom of the rulers, be they kings or the people speaking through representatives. Historically what had stood in the way of the Christian Western nations (and Woolsey tended to concentrate on the Christian Powers) was the unyielding essential, sovereignty. Yet he urged his readers to believe that principles of a philosophical kind should, or was it could, have a corrective effect. "Natural justice," he argued, "knows nothing of a right of conquest in the broad sense of that term, that is, of mere superior force, carrying with it the license to appropriate territory, or destroy national life."[8] These were ideas with which Taft could readily identify, since their foundations were embedded in him by family life and exhortation.

Woolsey's approach to contemporary thinking and policy was certainly from an American perspective on international relations. His extended discussion of rights and obligations bears this out. From the emergence of the nation-state in Europe with the onset of the modern era, nations were often at war, conducting land and sea fighting in ways violating American colonial and later national rights. In as much as the rights of the United States as a neutral had been abused during the wars of the French Revolution and Napoleon, and quite possibly might be so affected by future European power struggles, what Woolsey wrote was bound to gain the attention of Taft and his fellow students. In keeping with the whole thrust of the book there was a very long review of the

evolving principles governing neutral rights in opposition to the practices of belligerents. The plain failure of the nations to agree in detail
regarding such rights forced Woolsey and his students to conclude that
international law was more tentative than constitutional or statute law,
and therefore was defective because there was no enforcing agency.
But there were sanctions that might be imposed to protect the sovereign interests of neutral nations. These included the "moral sentiment
of each and all the states which have consented to the existing" international law and practice. And from there Woolsey went on: "Great as
the evil of war is, it is not in the existing condition of mankind the greatest [evil]. . . . Nations are reformed by the sobering influences of war.
Nations are exalted by contending in war for something which is good.
Let not this dread sanction, then, be thought to be of no use. War often
cures the internal maladies which peace has fostered."[9] Every young
man Taft's age no doubt thought back to the Civil War when there was
a contending for something that was good, the preservation of the
Union and the freeing of the slaves. And no doubt Woolsey had that in
mind in writing as he had.

The direct impression Taft's study of *International Law* was to have
on his conduct of diplomacy is, of course, impossible to gauge. Yet there
was so much he would encounter in his handling of relations between
the United States and other nations, European but Asian as well, that
he would have a useful frame of reference as part of his overall approach
to understanding the issues at hand.

If Woolsey's book was a product of traditional scholarship the lectures of William Graham Sumner were very much a matter of the new
look in style and content. Sumner's modus operandi in the lecture hall
was to dogmatize the teachings of Herbert Spencer, who, in turn, had
given social applications to the findings of Charles Darwin. Sumner's
aim was to overpower the undergraduate mind as he preached (his early
training was in theology and before coming to Yale he was an ordained

Episcopal clergyman) the gospel of laissez-faire capitalism. "I regard economic forces as simply parallel to physical forces, arising just as spontaneously and naturally, following the sequence of cause and effect," he told his students. Or again, "the human race has made no step in the direction of civilization which has not been won by pain and distress. It wins no steps now without paying for it in sacrifices." All this and much more added up to Sumnerology, a naked emphasis on force, power, strength enough to survive while others perished, according to natural law.[10] Taft became at best a partially wrought Social Darwinist, but there would be found traces and more than traces in certain of his diplomatic tactics in dealing with small Central American countries.

At the 1878 Yale commencement exercises Taft delivered a typical senior oration, "The Professional and Political Prospects of the College Graduates," as salutatorian of his class. He dealt with political corruption, the abuses of governmental authority by the Republican party, and centralization of power brought on by the Civil War. "The Republican party has lost its grip on the affections of the people," he lamented. When times were good the people winked at Republican wickedness, but now that times were bad the party was judged and found wanting. Taft was especially hard on the Republican-controlled Congress that appeared to be passing laws in every direction. "We are the worst governed people because we are the most governed people," aptly summed up his position. Voicing opposition to soft money and other proposals from the "insane West," he expressed the hope that an educated and informed electorate would be able "to sweep back the tide." At bottom Taft expressed great faith in the Constitution and the Republic. "Discontent in France makes a riot, in America a political party. In France the Commune sought their ends by violence, in America a safety valve is found for dangerous mutterings in the ballot box." He discovered other safety valves in immigration, opportunity, and wealth. He termed wealth the "great civilizer and source of a nation's happiness." All in all, his words added up to a standard oration by expressing deep concern about the present and confidence in the future life of the nation. The address exhibited much that was declamatory but offered a reasoned assessment of the country's woes, if not a way to overcome them.[11]

Taft's affection for Yale notwithstanding, his decision to return to Cincinnati and pursue the study of law there was a wise and sensible one. The Cincinnati Law School was recognized as one of the best centers of preparation for a legal career. The Taft name was well-known in the city, and in the profession that could mean useful connections in the future. The men of the law Taft would be associating with, in many instances, would be graduates of the Law School, and some might on occasion be part-time faculty. Then there were private reasons to return to his hometown. He was a personable young man, it might be said he was an eligible bachelor, and Taft loved to socialize. He read some law over the summer of '78, spent time in his father's office, and began his formal legal studies that September.

The method of instruction at the Cincinnati Law School was entirely deductive. Lectures explicated the law, drawing principles from the inherited rules of the past that, it was clearly stated, must continue to be relied upon. In other words, the legal world was an ordered universe. Beyond lectures on contracts, property, tort, and white collar criminal law (such as fraud and embezzlement) students were expected to read treatises from Coke and Blackstone to more contemporary commentators, such as Austin's *Principles of Jurisprudence*, along with standard works on evidence and criminal law dealing with personal injury. The approach thus described enabled the student to grasp the large outline of the law, giving him a feel for the history of its growth and development, an ordered phenomenon.

For Taft and his fellow students formal instruction was only part of their training. The practical side was learned by entering a law office to work as a kind of apprentice. But Taft's experience was different. Because his father was phasing out his legal practice under the pressure of public service in Washington, Will took a job as court reporter for Murat Halstead's Cincinnati Commercial. From this vantage point he came to understand the meaning of the law in the lives of everyday people. Offered permanent employment in the newspaper business he told friends he had taken the job simply to learn more about the workings of the justice system.[12]

Taft had entered upon the practice of law at a time when it was both hidebound in nature and also subject to challenge for that very reason. There was one very crucial particular, the sacredness of private property. Given the reigning materialism of the times, ownership of private property became a natural right and could not on that account be interfered with by the laws of the states or of the national government. The 14th Amendment stated that "no state shall deprive a person of property without due process of law," and as such was an echo of the 5th Amendment of the Bill of Rights. By the mid-1880s federal and state courts had ruled that "due process" was more than a procedural protection to ownership of private property; it had become a substantive right and therefore beyond the reach of government. Laissez-faire capitalism was enshrined in law.

The importance of property and successive alterations in society growing out of the Darwinian struggle for survival were familiar enough as a result of Taft's encounters with Professor Sumner at Yale. There were aspects of Sumner's philosophy that encouraged him to embrace notions of the extreme of property rights, but there were equally strong reasons why, ultimately, he would reject a system of ethics based on force. A passion for righteousness derived from his New England inheritance was no small consideration in his total outlook. At this early date

Taft was not a legal scholar but an avid learner respecting the detailed procedures of the law and its functioning. Very much occupied with studying the trees, he had not yet undertaken to view the forest in its fullest meaning.

Once graduated from law school and admitted to the bar in 1880 he was free to move in one of two directions. Legal practice was the more conventional route to take, but the pending retirement of his father worked to discourage him in that prospect. Besides, there was that deep-rooted and growing desire to be an officer of the court and not an advocate before the court. Drawing on his experiences as a court reporter and encouraged by the contacts he was able to make in political community, he was offered and accepted the position of Assistant Prosecutor for Hamilton County; Cincinnati was the county seat. This was an exceptional opportunity to take in the workings of the court system, seeing it from the inside. At this early stage Taft also began to take an active part in Ohio politics. His father had been defeated for the Republican nomination for the governorship in 1879, but he continued to be highly regarded by the party. His son's career doubtlessly benefited on that account. Being the honest man he was, the senior Taft felt it incumbent upon him to warn the political neophyte concerning the corruption William Howard would soon encounter, and to have no hand in it.

The young Taft somehow managed to stand sufficiently aloof from the Republican machine, quickly establishing his reputation as an honest politician. He never alienated himself from the party bosses to the degree that his chances of political preferment were endangered, however. Personally honest, he was at the same time politically realistic. The bosses, in turn, used the reputations of the Tafts, father and son, to their own advantage when it came to persuading voters of the character of Ohio Republicanism. After only a year as Assistant Prosecutor, and as if he was playing the political game, he became United States

Collector of Revenue for the First Ohio District. The appointment was made by President Arthur in keeping with his desire for clean government in the wake of Garfield's assassination. Loyalty to both the President and the party go a long way toward explaining Taft's willingness to take the Collector assignment. Not surprisingly he found himself ill-suited to the job as he came to realize how one's integrity could be so readily compromised. Upon his resignation he turned to the practice of law, all the while remaining politically in the swim. He campaigned for Joseph B. Foraker in his bid to become the governor of Ohio and for James G. Blaine (though he preferred Arthur) for the presidency in 1884. Both men lost their races but Taft gained stature and another political appointment in 1885, Assistant County Solicitor. When Foraker won the two-year term as governor in 1885 he rewarded Taft, who had supported him a second time, by naming him a judge of the Superior Court of Ohio to fill out an unexpired term. It was Judge Taft, now; he was not yet thirty years of age. At the next election he won the judgeship in his own right. It was clear to him how political activism was the surest road to judicial office.

In the meantime Taft had married. Will and Nellie had first met in 1884, and within the year he had become her ardent suitor. But Helen Herron was not minded to marry, fearing that she would have to forego her own ambitions for worldly success and recognition in the bargain. Helen (Nellie) Herron was the daughter of a well-respected Cincinnati lawyer, a personal friend of President Hayes, certainly acquainted with Alphonso Taft. Nellie was cultured and intelligent as well as pretty and popular. Often found in her father's law office she thought seriously of becoming a lawyer, but females were rarities indeed in the profession. The romance of Will and Nellie had a bookish tinge. They often met at the Mercantile Library and found themselves enjoying the same books, William Dean Howell's *Their Wedding Journey* and George Eliot's *Mill On The Floss*, among many others. Or they studied some of the great lives of the past, Franklin, Luther, Burke, Voltaire in particular appealed to them. Once married Nellie transposed her own ambitions to her husband's career. With her father she had once visited President and Mrs. Hayes in the White House and said openly that one day she, too, might be first lady. To her the judicial branch of government was dull, and surely did not seem to lead in the direction of the White House. Nellie would have much preferred to see her husband in the political arena with its excitement and rewards. To a significant degree she was to be the woman behind the President. Her influence stemmed from her own force of character and because her husband remained deeply in love with her.[13]

In the years 1885-1900 Taft was completely absorbed by the law as Ohio judge, as Solicitor General of the United States, and as a federal judge for the 6th circuit court of appeals. Except for his two-year stint in Washington, 1890-92, Nellie Taft would have to be content as the wife of a distinguished public servant in the confines (as she judged it) of Cincinnati. With three children to raise she still made time to read widely and hope for a more exciting future as her husband's career showed greater promise.

The same years were full of commotion and turmoil across the nation as the masses labored uneasily with the weight placed on their shoulders by the classes. Class warfare, of course, never seriously threatened the Republic, but discontent on farm and in factory came increasingly to dominate national and local politics. The Populist Movement was afoot in Kansas. Mary K. Lease urged farmers to raise more hell and less corn; Ignatius Donnelly in Minnesota accused the system of endemic corruption and included the courts in his bill of particulars. Beyond the Mississippi farmers looked increasingly to the Populist Party as a means of protecting them from neglect and of promoting their welfare. In 1892 Col. James B. Weaver of Iowa ran for president and garnered a million votes. At least twelve congressmen identified themselves as Populists when the 57th Congress convened. But it fell to William Jennings Bryan to capture the spirit of discontent and co-opt it in the name of the Democratic Party. Bryan became a prophet of doom for men of property, judges and otherwise, William Howard Taft among them. He discerned a threat to law and order when the rule of private property was at any time under the gun.

Equally, if not more disturbing to Taft, was the rising tide of unrest, expressed in strike action, which was evident wherever factories, mines, and railroads employed an expanding work force, skilled and unskilled. The major industrial disputes between capital and labor included the International Harvester confrontation in 1886, the Homestead workers' challenge to the Carnegie Steel Company over wages and working conditions in 1892, and the Pullman strike of 1894 (which was to involve Taft in his capacity as a federal appeals judge). All of these carried seeds of class warfare, distinctly so, in contrast to the Populist revolt. In the view of the courts not only capitalism but the Constitution was under fire. As a sitting judge, but no less than as solicitor general, Taft had learned a great deal about people, as opposed to corporations, lessons he was able to draw on once he was installed as governor of the Philippines. A feeling of compassion toward the under-class, a feature of his Island administration, really was given birth in public affairs as he came to see "the other side" in cases where the best interest of individuals was pitted against business practices. Typically he favored the rights of the propertied, yet cases in which he favored the individual should not be interpreted as lapses; they were correctives to what most judges treated as the absolute right to use property in order to maximize profits.[14]

Two cases in particular reveal differing outlooks on the rights of property under the law. In *Moores & Company v. Bricklayers Union No. 1* (1890), Taft displayed not only an unyielding position in favor of capital over labor, but he also chose to embrace a double standard of social morality. The dispute involved a secondary boycott by bricklayers who refused to handle any materials brought to the building site by various suppliers until their grievances were satisfied. One such supplier, Moores, sued the union for damages. Taft ruled that a secondary boycott was illegal, thereby upholding a lower court decision. But he went beyond the rule of law in handing down his opinion, arguing that malice was the motivation of the bricklayers. He could have arrived at that judgment only based on his private attitude toward the labor movement, relative to which he had deep suspicions that privately tended to demonize union leaders.[15] Some years later, when he was sitting for the 6th US court of appeals, Taft spoke out in favor of Narramore, a railroad brakeman, who had been so seriously injured on the job, that he required amputation of a leg. Narramore sued the railroad in federal court claiming contributary negligence on the part of the corporation, which had argued that Narramore was aware of the risks involved in his work and his injuries were due to his carelessness. Taft judged the matter differently, holding the railroad liable. But it should be noted the judgment was in favor of an individual and not in favor of a labor organization. It should also be noted that such cases came later in his time on the bench, toward the close of his judicial tenure.[16]

In the fall of 1889 a vacancy occurred on the Supreme Court and there was talk, and support from Ohio governor Foraker, in behalf of Taft to join the Court. In fact his name was submitted, along with others, to President Harrison for consideration. But his assessment of his prospects for such an appointment was realistic, writing his father: "My chances of going to the moon and of donning a silk gown at the hands of President Harrison are about equal." He himself recognized that he was too young, just thirty-two at the time, and with limited judicial experience, and none of it dealing with federal law. Instead, the President named him Solicitor General of the United States, a relatively new office; Taft was only the second man to hold that post.[17]

At first he was unsure if he should accept the appointment since it meant giving up his position on the Ohio Superior Court and leaving Cincinnati. Nellie and the family in general advised him to seize the opportunity to be in the nation's capital and to argue cases before the Supreme Court. Flattered to be that well-regarded he put aside misgivings about the demands of office. It proved an ideal opportunity to renew and deepen his study of the history and workings of constitutional law, so his two years as the government's chief advocate became an important phase in his ongoing legal education. Altogether he was to argue twenty-seven cases before the high court, winning all but seven, thereby earning something of a national reputation for the cogency of his briefs.

As Solicitor General, Taft's most notable success came in the *Bering Sea Case* in 1891. At issue was the taking of seals from the Bering Sea by Canadian fishermen in an area where the United States claimed jurisdiction. With the acquisition of Alaska, Americans began to treat the Bering Sea as *mare clausam*. American sealers refused to abide by the commonly agreed-upon three-mile limit. Furthermore the United States authorized its revenue cutters to seize vessels intruding in the area. Great Britain launched vigorous protests beginning in 1885, but to no avail. Friction between London and Washington mounted in consequence. A flash point was reached when a Canadian-owned ship, *W.P. Sayward*, was taken into port, and the federal district court sitting in Alaska ordered it sold for violating American waters inside the three-mile limit. Great Britain entered a suit at law against the United States government, thereby requiring the Department of Justice through the voice of the Solicitor General to argue the case before the Supreme Court. The weight of Taft's brief rested on his contention that the judicial branch could not under the Constitution order the executive branch to cease and desist in the use of revenue cutters, whose authority derived from the Treasury Department. Such an action, if allowed, would go directly against the separation of powers principle. The Supreme Court ruled in favor of Taft's well-crafted brief as constitutionally sound. For the first time in his experience constitutional law and international law intersected. He came to know, in the barest kind of way, how the law of nations might impact on his own nation.[18]

Another case, more typical of the litigation undertaken by the Solicitor General, dealt with the issue of the legality of the collection of customs under the McKinley Tariff. The issue at law was whether the tariff act had been passed constitutionally in as much as the Speaker of the House had counted the vote of numerous representatives as present though they had taken no part in the vote. The Court decided such members could be included to make up the necessary quorum. Taft's brief again had much to do with the Court's ruling. The large result of his work in this advocacy office was that he became well known to the Court as a lawyer of standing, both by reason of the depth and thoroughness of his arguments and by his courtroom decorum. He also had become a trusted colleague of the Attorney General, W.H. Miller, which added to his reputation on the Washington scene. All of this made it more than likely he would again be in Washington in some higher capacity as the years went by. Few things would have pleased Nellie Taft more than to be among what she termed "the bigwigs" in the nation's capital.

There was more to being in Washington than Taft's work as the country's chief barrister. Opportunity was his to meet and become friends with the next generation of Republican leaders, including Theodore Roosevelt, then a member of the United States Civil Service Commission, Henry Cabot Lodge, a rising politico, Thomas Reed, Speaker of the House, John Hay, future Secretary of State, and that list is far from complete. True, Taft kept his distance from GOP politics while insuring the perception that he was a reliable party member.

Taft's friendship with Theodore Roosevelt had untold consequences, both short term and long term. It should be thought of as the decisive friendship in his public career. Their fellowship began on a positive note, thrived for many years, gave Taft the Republican nomination for the presidency in 1908, a virtual guarantee the White House was his. By 1910 their falling out commenced over Taft's presidential policies and his actions. The split became a total one in 1912 when Roosevelt was outmaneuvered at the Republican nomination convention. The two men differed sharply when it came to planning for world peace in the aftermath of World War I in what was a duel between their two opposed versions of where America was to figure in the postwar settlement.[19]

Upon first meeting in Washington in 1890 the two young idealists discovered they had much in common by way of background and public philosophy. They were "goo-goo," in the phrase of the day, a derision aimed at advocates of good government. Taft as solicitor general held the higher position, TR being but one member of the Civil Service Commission. When McKinley won the presidential race in 1896 and was forming a cabinet, Roosevelt called upon Taft to use his influence with his fellow Ohioan to be named Assistant Navy Secretary. TR was so named, the very beginning of a spectacular rise to power and a career that, in due season, would prove very beneficial to Judge Taft.

In March, 1892, the Congress acted to provide one additional judge for each of the federal circuit courts. The timing could not have been better for Taft.[20] A successful solicitor, he really preferred a judgeship. His scent was up and support was widespread, from members of the Cincinnati bar to President Harrison himself who referred to him as someone who had shown that he possessed "judicial qualities of the highest order." There were no serious obstacles to his appointment as a circuit judge and sound political reason in its favor. Not even Nellie Taft's disappointment in leaving Washington was enough to persuade her husband to forego what was to him a rare opportunity, pregnant with the prospect of one day joining the justices on the high court, where he was respected for his jurisprudence. For any number of justices service on the circuit courts had been a stepping stone to the Supreme Court. Who could say, in 1893, as he began his tenure as an appeals judge, that one day Nellie Taft might mix with the Washington bigwigs after all.

Of the many cases Judge Taft ruled on in his eight years of office, none was as important or so revealing of his judicial philosophy as *In re: Phelan* (1894).[21] In that year, 1894, the American Railway Union, led by Eugene Debs, struck all trains in and out of Chicago that included Pullman cars in their make-up. This action was taken in sympathy with the workers at the Pullman Palace Car Company located in the company town of Pullman, Illinois. The company had drastically reduced wages without a compensatory reduction of rents and other necessities of life in company-owned houses and stores. In effect what the American Railway Union had done was to institute a secondary boycott by taking action against railroad companies that were innocent parties. President Cleveland employed the military to break the strike. Privately Taft professed nothing but contempt bordering on hatred for the striking workers. Writing to his wife in July, 1894, he saw "affairs in Chicago seeming to be much disturbed. It will be necessary for the military to kill some of the mob before the trouble can be stayed." And again: "They have killed six of the workers as yet. This is hardly enough to make an impression."[22] Yet when the case growing out of the Pullman strike came before Taft, the judge allowed none of his personal rancor to influence his opinion.

In defiance of a federal injunction Debs had ordered Frank Phelan to go to Cincinnati with the purpose of encouraging railway workers there to defy the injunction and spread the strike. Phelan was found in contempt of court and ordered to jail. Taft referred to the sentencing as "a most disagreeable duty." Yet given his public philosophy, as he stated it, "if the orders of the court are not obeyed, the next step is unto anarchy." Nonetheless, his opinion in *In re: Phelan*, stated clearly and fully that labor had the right to strike, to organize, to accumulate funds, all essential weapons to use in the struggle with capitalism. The common law had long held that labor must be free to sell its services, but resort to a secondary boycott went beyond the legal rights of organized labor. In a sense Taft had brought labor unions out from the shadows of illegality into the clear light of protection under law. Taft's assertions in this respect were all the more noteworthy given the pronounced anti-labor attitude of the corporations and the classes. In light of further evidence Taft was beginning to evolve from a strict construction of constitutional protection of private property to a somewhat pragmatic construction in which rulings might be based, to some extent at least, on the effects produced. His position in the *Addystone Pipe and Steel* case (1898) bears this out. He invoked the Sherman Anti-Trust Act, pointing out that Addystone had fixed prices in restraint of trade, and he thereby challenged the 1895 Supreme Court ruling in the E.C. Knight Case. More surprising still, the high court affirmed Taft's decision in a rare application of the anti-trust law. Corporate rights were not sacrosanct after all. Meanwhile, in 1896, Taft became Dean of the Cincinnati Law School and Professor of Property, responsibilities that added to his sense of satisfaction about insuring the cause of law and order.

During his years as a federal appeals judge Taft had consolidated his understanding of the Constitution and the laws pursuant thereto. He was comfortable with his life both on and off the court. If he entertained any thoughts of advancement it would mean appointment to the Supreme Court. With the Republican party perennially in occupation of the White House and in the likelihood President McKinley would be re-elected to a second term in 1900, prospects for appointment to the high court, should an opening occur, were promising. When in January of 1900, well before election time, he was summoned to meet the President, he could only believe that his supreme ambition, to be a justice of the most renowned court in the nation, was to be realized. His surprise was total and his disappointment masked by strength of character when he was asked by McKinley to serve as a civil official in the Philippines. It was a decision he had to weigh carefully, taking into account various factors. How long would his tenure in the office be? Could he expect preferential consideration if, in a few years, a Supreme Court opening developed? As a man of judicial temperament and experience, could he honestly take on the kind of administrative duties governing would entail? How would his health respond to the climate of the Islands? Was this really the best way to serve his country? Finally, would his wife and family think well of such an assignment? All of these questions had to be addressed and answered positively if William Howard Taft would do the career about-face involved in accepting the presidential call and the personal challenge.

The meeting with the President was a historic one. Present were Secretary of War Elihu Root and Navy Secretary John Davis Long, their purpose being to help persuade the judge to accede to the president. Root was especially forceful, even demanding, because he sensed at once that Taft was cool to the very idea that the United States retain the Philippines. Taft appeared both innocent of the implications of retaining the Islands for America's world position and in fact, disinterested. Root probably was the one voice he would listen to and the Secretary of War made bold to insist that Taft join the commission being formed to administer the new possession, and that he would likely be its head, before being officially designated civil governor. It was further indicated that he would be in the Islands a year or so, and the President assured him in so many words that a Supreme Court appointment could follow once an opening occurred. Returning to Cincinnati he found his wife keen to have him agree to take the offer, and his brothers, Horace in particular, encouraged him in the same direction. But it was Taft's decision, convinced as he became of the need of the

United States, having insisted that Spain surrender its control of the archipelago, install a government that would bring law, order, and peace to the people, and with ongoing help from Washington, their economic well-being. For Taft this was a dazzling prospect and one in which, as it turned out, he attained his purpose.[23] His meeting with McKinley had taken place in January. By mid-April, 1900, the whole Taft family – wife and three children – accompanied him on his westward journey. After stops in Honolulu and Hong Kong, the future civil governor arrived in Manila, to be greeted by the senior American military commander General Arthur McArthur. The Ohio judge had become the first American proconsul. The pertinence of his legal/judicial experience is not necessarily self-evident, yet it was to have a pronounced and positive influence on his conduct of the proconsular office. From the onset of his assignment Taft conceived of his responsibilities as centered in nation building, a constitutional republic in form. To achieve this the majesty of the law was to be foremost, the lesson that Taft had promoted and practiced as a sitting judge. Without respect for the law anarchy would prevail, a condition that could not be overcome at the muzzle of a gun. And Taft had faith in the willingness and ability of the Filipino people, properly schooled, to become the first self-governing nation in east Asia. Rarely have passion, Taft's total commitment to a government of laws and not of men, and practicality, the American governmental model seeded and growing in the minds of the Island people, mated so productively.

NOTES

[1] For an overview of the Gilded Age and after, consult Vincent DeSantis, *The Shaping of Modern America, 1877-1916* (St. Louis: Forum Press, 1977).

[2] On the larger theme of order, see Robert H. Wiebe, *The Search for Order* (New York: Hill & Wang, 1984).

[3] Richard Hofstadter, *Social Darwinism in American Thought* (Boston: Beacon Press, 1969). See also Ralph H. Gabriel, *The Course of American Democratic Thought* (New York: Ronald Company, 1940).

[4] David Healy, *Expansionism: The Imperialist Urge in the 1890s* (Madison: University of Wisconsin Press, 1970) offers a somewhat visceral account.

[5] "Alphonso Taft," *American National Dictionary* (New York: Oxford University Press, 1990) vol. IX, pp. 264-65.

[6] William Howard Taft to Henry W. Taft, Jan. 23, 1899, in Henry F. Pringle, *The Life and Times of William Howard Taft*, 2 vols. (New York: Farrar & Rinehart, 1932) I, 43. For an insightful analysis of Taft and Unitarianism consult Edward H. Cotton, *William Howard Taft: A Character Study* (Boston: Beacon Press, 1932), pp. 75-78.

[7] David H. Burton discusses Taft's Yale days in *The Learned Presidency* (Madison, NJ: Fairleigh Dickinson University Press, 1988), pp. 91-96.

[8] Theodore D. Woolsey, *Introduction to the Study of International Law* (New York: Charles Scribner's Sons, 1877), pp. 5, 21.

[9] Woolsey, *International Law*, pp. 407-08.

[10] For an understanding of Sumner there are two vintage biographies: Albert G. Keller, *Reminiscences of William Graham Sumner* (New Haven: Yale University Press, 1927), and Harris E. Starr, *William Graham Sumner* (New York: Henry Holt, 1925). To sample Sumner's message and its dogmatism, see William Graham Sumner, *Earth-Hunger and Other Essays* (New Haven: Yale University Press, 1939).

[11]   Yale College Records, Yale University Archives.

[12]   Pringle, *Taft*, I, 50.

[13]   Judith I. Anderson, *William Howard Taft, an Intimate History* (New York: W.W. Norton, 1981), pp. 51-52.

[14]   Robert C. McMath, *American Populism* (New York: Hill & Wang, 1993) studies Populism as a period phenomenon.

[15]   45 *Federal Reporter*, 730-45.

[16]   96 *Federal Reporter*, 216; Nell Painter, *Standing at Armageddon: United States, 1877-1919* (New York: W.W. Norton, 1989) looks at the period from a labor point of view.

[17]   Pringle, *Taft*, I, 107-09.

[18]   Herbert Duffy, *William Howard Taft* (New York: Minton, Balch and Co., 1930), pp. 29-30; Charles S. Campbell, "The Bering Sea Settlement of 1892," *Pacific Historical Review*, XXXII (Nov., 1963), pp. 34-67.

[19]   William Manners, *TR and Will* (New York: Harcourt Brace, 1969) traces the breakdown of their relationship.

[20]   62 *Federal Reporter*, 802-23.

[21]   Pringle, *Taft*, I, 128.

[22]   85 *Federal Reporter*, 271.

[23]   Ralph E. Minger, *William Howard Taft and American Foreign Policy: The Apprenticeship Years, 1900-1908* (Urbana: University of Illinois Press, 1975) has the best account, pp. 1-6.

2 . LEARNING CURVE

When William Howard Taft came to the presidency in 1909 no prior occupant of that office had had the range of diplomatic experience that he possessed. His eight years as civil governor of the Philippines and then as secretary of war had taught him the practice of diplomacy; for him it was now something of an art. At first glance it might be argued that once he was in the White House Taft was merely following orders given him by President McKinley, Secretary of War Elihu Root, and Theodore Roosevelt. A closer look shows that in the shaping of a Far Eastern policy for the United States, Taft put down the foundation by negotiating the Taft-Katsura Agreement, as well as doing the spade work for the Root-Takahira Agreement. In 1906 an internal political upheaval threatened in Cuba. Roosevelt was moved to exasperation— "I would like to wipe the Cubans off the face of the map"—and dispatched Taft to handle the crisis. The diplomat in action brought the warring sides together and ordered U.S. troops to remain in the island as a guarantee of law and order. Consider, seriatim, Taft's diplomatic record, to be reviewed in depth: dealing with a colonial nation while in the Philippines, with the Vatican over the friars' land issue, with Panama at the start of the construction of the canal, with Cuba, and with Japan as a matter of balance of power in the Far East. The learning curve was a long and sweeping one, a remarkable preparation for dealing with the diplomatic opportunities that would be his while serving as president.

At the close of the nineteenth century the American government, not to say the American people, was not ready or, as some critics insisted, was not suited to become a player in the diplomatic chess game of power politics in East Asia. Yet the year 1898 had borne witness to the unassailable fact that the United States had become a Pacific power by the annexation of the Hawaiian Islands and the decision to acquire the

Philippines in the wake of the Spanish American War. The outcome of that war had brought to a head in dramatic fashion the various forces, prospects, and ideologies building up in the 1890s. All of a sudden, the republic had become an imperial democracy.

The great prize luring the industrialized nations of Europe and the new Japan, emerging as rival to the Western countries, was China. Its vast resources of raw materials and its huge population as a potential market for manufactured goods constituted the China trade. Now the United States seemed destined to join the pack quarreling over control of China, which in the long run could lead to war among the powers. The sheer number of nations on the prowl for advantage in the exploitation of the China trade called for a diplomacy based on balance of power. The British, Germans, French, Russians, Japanese, and now Americans—no one of these was prepared to allow the others to dominate China commercially or otherwise. Yet the Americans, the newcomers on the scene, were at a disadvantage, having neither leaseholds nor extraterritorial privileges in China, which at the time was but a half-wrought nation.[1]

To the Americans what was called for was an "open door" with all the competing nations enjoying equal access to all the spoils of diplomacy. In 1899 Secretary of State John Hay announced a version of this open door concept, the first of two notes setting forth the position of the United States. In tone it was nothing less than magnanimous. It read in effect: the government of the United States would be pleased to secure assurances from other interested powers that each within its respective spheres of influence will in no way interfere with any treaty port or vested interest within any so-called sphere of interest or leased territory it may have in China.[2] But Hay's intention was altogether self-serving. The note was circulated to the appropriate foreign ministries from London to Tokyo without tangible effect. As one cynic observed the lack of enthusiasm was dictated by the implied request that all the thieves in the room should stand up.

Meanwhile the Boxer Rebellion broke out in 1900, an abortive effort on the part of students, intellectuals, and assorted other Chinese, designed to throw off the economic-geographic yoke in the name of a free and sovereign China. The rebellion was put down by a combined military operation of the Powers, an action in which United States troops were a part. Then in July 1900, Secretary Hay issued a second Open Door Note, one of the most remarkable policy statements for a new century. It was prompted by American apprehensions that the military contingents of the various powers called in to destroy the Boxer Movement would stay in place in their respective leaseholds, thereby carving China into so many colonies. This second note stated that the United States declared itself in favor of the "territorial integrity" of China, a policy intended to ward off any attempt to colonize. The United States thereby appeared committed to a major role in Far Eastern affairs.[3]

The appointment of William Howard Taft as head of the second Philippines Commission, and presently to be its first civil governor, had two objectives in the thinking of McKinley. It was generally agreed that political stability in the islands was a precondition for American commercial success in China. Manila was to be the great entrepôt for east-west trade. Taft first focused on the problem of law and order; it was his grand objective since it met the most pressing need for Filipino society. In so proceeding he came to understand that he was governing a colonial nation demanding of him the skill of a diplomat as well as that of an administrator. In meeting this responsibility his work as the diplomat and the administrator tended to meld. Only by proceeding as the representative of a great nation to a fledgling nation could needed reforms be brought about. Nothing that Taft did as civil governor spells this out more clearly than his push to assemble an all-Filipino congress at the earliest possible date. It may be argued in consequence that Taft's all around success as governor solidified the United States, both as a trading nation and as an increasingly influential voice in the international politics of the region.

If in the eyes of the McKinley administration the Philippines constituted a colonial nation, for many Filipinos their country continued to be a ward of old-style imperialism and they were determined to free themselves from foreign domination. As in Cuba during the 1880s and before, the people of the islands dreamed of independence. No one personified this commitment better than José Rizal. Born in Laguna province in 1835, he was awarded M.D. and Ph.D. degrees by the University of Madrid in the mid-1880s. While living in Europe Rizal published his widely acclaimed book, *Noli me tangere*, published in English as *The Lost Eden* in 1886. In it he attacked both the Spanish civil administration and the religious orders of his native land. A second novel, *El Filibusterismo*, restated his opposition to government and church in 1891, and he returned to Manila the next year. Almost immediately he was arrested as an agitator and banished from the capital. On his way to Cuba in 1896 he was intercepted by the police and summarily executed as an enemy of the state.[4] Rizal's martyrdom incited a full scale rebellion against the tyrannous mother country. The rebel movement was making only limited headway by 1898 and the outbreak of the Spanish-American War. But the fuse was burning. One of the most important leaders in the drive for independence was Emilio Aguinaldo. He and his followers were led to understand, or led themselves to believe, that the American victory at the battle of Manila Bay signified Philippine independence. Armed Filipino irregulars had assisted American troops in taking Manila City and environs, which meant the collapse of Spanish rule. When McKinley made the decision to retain the whole of the archipelago, as stated in the Peace of Paris of 1898, the independence movement flared up with its fire aimed at the American occupiers. Implementation of stated American policy was at a crossroads. The United States could simply withdraw from this greatest of colonial ventures, as many anti-imperialists at home were demanding, or pour enough troops into the Islands to scatter the Filipino forces now under the command of Aguinaldo. For more than a year prior to Taft's arrival in Manila in July 1900, a guerilla war raged, an ugly bushwhacking struggle between two equally determined foes. Gen. Elwell Otis, the U.S. commander, believed in scorching the earth, destroying villages, shooting unarmed civilians—a brutal effort to break the back of the resistance. Otis was relieved of his command and replaced by Gen. Arthur MacArthur who believed, to a degree, in a carrot and stick method of subduing the Filipinos. He announced a general amnesty just two months before Taft was in residence. As he phrased it: "a complete amnesty for the past and liberty for the future." From mid-1900 on, with a responsible military commander and a forward-looking civilian administrator, the McKinley administration promised a resolution of the paradox, namely, that it must apply force majeur to subduing a people so that it might enjoy the blessing of liberty. General Otis's tactics had shown how severe American repression could be. Judge Taft must demonstrate how constructive and promising American civil rule could be. From the very beginning of his time in the Islands, Taft was determined that only by treating the inhabitants there, one and all, as equals—in his world that meant as citizens in a self-governing state in the making—could the large policy of the United States be realized.

Taft's diplomacy went hand in hand with the economic, social, and political reforms that he deemed necessary. Schools must be established to promote literacy, clinics opened to meet basic health needs, roads built to promote commerce, units of local government encouraged to begin to teach the lessons of self-rule, land reforms carried out to give to the average farmer a stake in society. To bring all this about, well-trained and dedicated Americans must join hands with their Filipino counterparts while Governor Taft lent support.[5]

Nations cannot be made overnight and colonies historically have often remained colonies, especially if the population is distinct in race and culture from the dominant country. In the Philippines it becomes essential, therefore, to appreciate how Taft went about bridging the divide between the conquerors and the conquered and in consequence how he prepared the Filipino people to become citizens of an emerging nation-state. Undoubtedly this is what President McKinley had in mind when in 1898 he appointed the Schurman Commission to make an assay of the raw material at hand for constituting a Filipino nation. That commission's report, given to the President in 1899, was most encouraging. But McKinley himself had no real grasp of what this would entail and how it could be done. In casting about for a civil governor he told one friend he wanted a man who was "stern, honest, tactful, a man of education and executive ability, a man who was fearless but conservative and who would get along with the people."[6] These were more than descriptive adjectives, with the exception of his perceived need to have a governor who would endeavor to get along with the Filipinos themselves. In fact he got such a man not alone in the person but in the personality of William Howard Taft. During his stay in the Islands Taft proved to be warmhearted, cheerful, optimistic, positive, and charming in combination with all the attributes McKinley had wished for. A sociable gentleman in Cincinnati and in Washington, he was completely at ease in meeting the established families of the land. Equally significant he was open and available to people from all walks of life. The very fact that he had brought his wife and three children with him to Manila was a sign that he came not to rule but to help the people to learn to govern themselves.

In the matter of nation building Taft was strongly influenced, one might say determined, by the American governmental model. To him the Philippines was a "great experimental laboratory of practical government." The United States, that is, the federal union, appealed to him as a kind of blueprint. After all, the people of the aspiring nation were widely scattered over many islands, living in different provinces; therefore provinces might well function as "states" in a federation, sending representatives to an all-Filipino congress. Such a representative body was the very thing Taft worked to bring about. The erection of provincial and central agencies of governing required, in Taft's judgment, a worthwhile civil service. It was to be established in law, whereby officials from top to bottom must meet certain criteria, and the application standards must be strictly adhered to. Such an arrangement was foreign to the old Spanish methods of governing. The people would now be assured that this new government was intended as an instrument of rule accessible to the full range of people who would be governors and governed alike.[7]

The task of Taft and his fellow commissioners in creating the formalities of this new national political structure had, of necessity, to include revisions of the civil and criminal law codes. Judge Taft, to revert to his time as a federal appeals court magistrate, was totally dissatisfied with the justice system in place since it was staffed by native born judges relying on Spanish judicial procedures. A new system of justice demanded new judges, both along the lines of an American model. Taft put the matter directly: "We cannot make satisfactory courts unless we appoint American judges in most cases in order that by example these people know what Anglo-Saxon justice means." He pleaded with his judicial brethren in the United States to recommend "upright lawyers with at least ten years experience, who will make good judges . . . and who have a sufficient knowledge of Spanish to enable them to carry on a court in that language." Taft held firmly to the view that for an emerging nation, the appearance as well as the reality of justice must be assured in order to win acceptance by Filipinos of all ranks. He believed this could be accomplished by judges of high moral character without resorting to a jury system. The literacy level of the general population was such that jury trials were impractical.[8]

How to solve the problem of illiteracy was much on Taft's mind as he sought to place piece after piece of a detailed design of rule into a functional relationship. Progress was sure to be slow. Under the direction of Frederick W. Atkinson, his Secretary of Education, schools were built and scores of young Americans, earnest men and women, were recruited to take their places in the classrooms. Filipinos were enthusiastic about the prospect of education but the process was complicated by the need to know basic English. Nonetheless, a willingness of the American teachers was matched by the eagerness of the Filipinos to learn. The net effect stood in such marked contrast to Spanish indifference toward education for the ordinary people that a genuinely friendly relationship grew up between the islanders and their partners in progress. In addition to a Department of Education other bureaus, including Health, Forestry, Agriculture, and Customs were part of Governor Taft's efforts to plan for the future of the Philippines.[9]

William Howard Taft as civil governor put into place the basic ingredients necessary for the Filipinos to build their own nation. At the same time he had, by force of character and commitment, breathed life into these formalities. Political structure, a legal system, and an educational administration exceeded the expectations of McKinley, Root, and Roosevelt, while at the same time he spiked the guns of the anti-imperialist naysayers.

Much of the success of the Taft administration derived from the power he enjoyed on site and the staunch support he received from Washington. Proconsul and presidents were in sync. Yet in the matter of the friars' lands, the disposition of the land, that is, the governor's hands were tied. And there is a certain irony here because there was no denying that the several religious orders held legal title to 400,000 acres of arable land. Taft, of course, was ultrasensitive to the rights of property owners, whereever and whoever they were.

For the United States to claim the land under the rule of eminent domain was unthinkable to him and to the Roosevelt administration.

From earliest times the Filipinos had been converted to Roman Catholicism by the Spanish conquerors. And they remained, in large part, faithful to the Church despite the abuses perpetrated by the religious orders. The people working the land were virtually serfs. Furthermore since the friars were all Spanish—little effort was made to train a native clergy—their influence with colonial rule was out of all proportion to their religious calling. These conditions, which were centuries old, became more and more onerous by the year the United States took over the Islands. José Rizal, it will be recalled, denounced the abuses of both church and state in his writings which made him their enemy and led to his execution. Making peace with the church over this issue promised to require deft diplomacy. Taft was ready to recommend one or more lawyer/diplomats and was especially keen to send John W. Foster. He had been President Harrison's Secretary of State and knew the whys and wherefores of international affairs. Once the question of ownership was settled the American plan was to sell small tracts of land to individual farmers, men who had already worked the land, on easy financial terms. The plan was intended to serve as the economic foundation, the stake in society principle, for the political structure.[10]

Governor Taft returned to the United States in late 1901 to testify before the Senate Committee on the Philippines. In his testimony he argued that education for all the people went hand in hand with land ownership and was therefore a key part of the total proposition of mentoring a nation in the making. Education, he reported, was moving along slowly, but land reform would require a treaty with the Vatican. At this stage Taft did not expect to be named to undertake the mission to Rome, having no great enthusiasm for it. Nonetheless President Roosevelt decided on Taft, believing that Taft and only Taft could

resolve the issue to the satisfaction of both parties. He was instructed
by Secretary of War Root that his visit to the Vatican was in no way an
act of official diplomacy; rather it was a business deal pure and simple,
a negotiation leading to the purchase of the friars' lands. In fact, the
mission turned out to be both diplomacy and business. The two were
so intertwined they defied separation. Once at the Vatican Taft was
received by the papal Secretary of State, Cardinal Rampolla who
presented him to Pope Leo XIII with all the formality associated with
diplomatic protocol. And Taft seemed altogether at ease under the
circumstances in which he found himself. The Pope was receptive to
the idea of the sale of the lands in question if a price could be agreed
upon. But like most absolute rulers, he had to take into consideration
the powerful interests of the heads of the religious orders. They
argued against the American offer, fearing that the money received
would be funds added to the ecclesiastical treasury rather than to the
religious congregations involved. It was the Peter and Paul dilemma
complicated by a lack of consensus on the amount of money on offer.
The Americans proposed to pay $5 million in gold, just half of what the
Vatican expected. Taft had been instructed by Root to propose "full
and fair compensation," and both men found the $10 million expect-
ed by the Vatican "excessive." The American fall-back proposal was to
establish an arbitration tribunal. This body would come together in
Milan, take evidence, and render a decision about price. It became
clear as a result of conversations that two sticking points surfaced, the
price and the departure of the Spanish religious orders from the
Philippines, to be replaced by American priests who, in addition to
serving the people, would begin training a native clergy. Taft left
Rome without an agreement but he believed that progress had been
made. The ice had been broken, he reported: "we shall have considerably less difficulty here in making Rome understand the situation."
Within a year and a half a deal was finalized. Three hundred thousand

acres were purchased at a cost of $7,543,000. Within a decade 50,000 property-owning farmers were at work, and theirs was a stake in society. Taft was delighted with the outcome since it fitted perfectly into his prescription for peace and prosperity for the Philippines in the years to come.[11]

The larger question remained. Having brought about tangible improvements in the Filipino way of life, gifts as it were, given by the American government and people as a means of pacifying the Islands, the United States could proceed safely and surely in pursuit of the China trade. So long as successive administrations in Washington were minded to remain active in the affairs of the Far East, Washington would be in possession of a reliable dependency. But to add another dimension, should the Filipinos mature and grow in the direction of self-government, thereby attaining true nationhood, the United States would have a friend and ally. Granted the prospect of full independence was in the distant future, Taft heartily endorsed the proposition that one people cannot give another people the gift of self-rule. He believed that it could take as many as fifty years (and he was about right in his estimate), but he could not have imagined that, vital to Filipino independence, years of wartime suffering under Japanese occupation would take place. For the moment and the foreseeable future, the Ohio judge, as administrator and diplomat, had accomplished much in terms of personal growth, as well as positioning the United States as a regional power in the Far East.

In broad perspective Theodore Roosevelt was his own secretary of state. He acquired the canal zone, added a corollary to the Monroe Doctrine, managed to settle the Alaska boundary dispute, involved the United States in the Algeciras Conference of 1906, and helped to bring an end to the Russo-Japanese War in 1905. Nonetheless amidst this flurry of diplomatic activity he found it useful to him and his overall policy outlook to call on his secretary of war, a position Taft had held from 1904, to act as a troubleshooter in Panama, in Cuba, and in the Far East, all the while trusting his steady hand in directing progress in the Philippines towards nationhood. The President so readily appreciated Taft's skill in heading off trouble that his efforts in the field of foreign policy undoubtedly contributed to TR's decision to support him for the Republican nomination for the presidency in 1908.

In May 1904, Roosevelt informed Taft that "all work in the digging, construction and completion of the canal, and all governmental power in and over said Canal Zone . . . shall be carried on or exercised under your supervision as Secretary of War."[12]   Given this mandate, Taft once again had to combine administrative know-how with diplomatic skill in order to achieve the desired result, namely, completion of the largest construction project in modern times. Until his assignment, work on the enterprise had been going slowly and uncertainly. It now became Taft's responsibility to get construction underway in earnest (administrative) and to do so without direct interference with the sovereignty of the Republic of Panama across whose territory the canal was being built (diplomatic).

Roosevelt's instruction to Taft in this latter regard was unambiguous. In part it read: "we have not the slightest intention of establishing an independent colony in the middle of the state of Panama. . . . Least of all do we desire to interfere with the business and prosperity of the people. . . . It is our full intention that the rights we exercise shall be exercised with all proper care for the honor and interests of the people of Panama."[13] In carrying out his dual duties Taft would be faced with a series of challenges, the first of which was to act, or to refrain from acting, in such a way as to preserve Panama's sovereignty in appearance and in reality. Fundamental to this was making decisions and/or arrangements that would maintain the economy on an even keel. As with most Caribbean nations, political instability was a lurking danger that the United States was not willing to tolerate, given the enormous investments in canal construction and equipment and national honor. Taft made this point in writing to his brother Charles: the Hay-Bunau-Varilla Treaty of 1903 "permits us to prevent revolutions, and I shall advise we will have no more. . . . We have four hundred marines and a fleet on one side and three naval vessels on the other." Tough talk, surely, but mostly talk as it turned out.[14]

As Taft once observed: "The problem of the canal is the problem of the excavation of a mass greater than ever before made in the history of the world." The project was awesome in scope. Materials of all kinds would have to be brought to the building sites, equipment coming in all sizes and shapes must be placed at hand for a work force of huge numbers, and for whom food, shelter, and basic health care must be provided. And all these elements must come together, synchronized as a team. At the same time Taft had to see to it that Panama, a tiny nation, would somehow survive the presence and the power of the United States on its land. The local economy required attention. Import taxes are ordinarily placed on goods coming into a country, in this case, the country of Panama. Yet the United States controlled the two ports of entry, Colon and Panama City. Were the various materials entering to come in duty free? If so, the local economy could soon be dragged down, and bring about political unrest. Such an interaction of events, needs, people, and priorities must not be allowed to play out.[15]

Taft was, in consequence, drawn into the political dissension arising in a conservative party, which he was ready to support, to prevent the upheaval likely to follow if the liberals came into power. The president of the republic, Amador, spoke for the Conservatives and General Huertas led the Liberals, composed mostly of workers and small tradesmen, groups that were in dire straits. Instinctively Taft wanted Amador to stay in office and was moved to impose a 10% ad valorem duty on all goods entering Panama; he deemed that a figure sufficient to keep the economy from collapse. Beyond that he was willing to raise the duty to 15% should the lower rate prove insufficient to satisfy the needs of the people in Panama. The fact to be noted is the full authority that the Secretary of War exercised. In the objective order it meant the sovereignty of the Republic was "titular." It came down to this: Panama, whether its government was conservative or liberal, was being ruled in some essentials by the United States. This was further spelled out by Taft's conduct of diplomatic relations between a semisovereign nation and a fully sovereign nation. He was known to refer to Panama as a "kind of Opera Bouffe republic and nation." And action would seem to have followed in the matter of sovereignty. What was important for the United States was that law and order were kept as long as the canal was being built, a project that continued through Taft's term as president. Administratively and diplomatically William Howard Taft had been instrumental in making the dirt fly in Panama.[16]

"Cuba Libre" was the cry resounding across America in 1898 as the United States went to war with Spain for the freedom and independence of the most important island in the Caribbean. And the Teller amendment to the Congressional declaration of war, to the disbelief of some of the European governments but to the satisfaction of the American people, announced that Cuba would indeed be free and independent once the war was won. The incongruity of this decision was deemed "curious" by outsiders. The Philippines, nine thousand miles away, were to undergo a "colonial phase" of many years duration while Cuba, just ninety miles off America, was to be recognized as a full-fledged nation. The reasons for this difference in approach to the spoils of war are easy to appreciate. The United States entered the 1898 war with the expressed purpose of freeing Cuba, and for the most part, the war was fought for Cuba and in Cuba. Possession of the Philippines, in contrast, was not part of the McKinley administration's thinking as the war got underway. The outcome of the battle of Manila Bay, per accidens, gave the United States the opportunity to control the whole archipelago. In the domestic political arena the advocates of imperialism (colonialism) outmaneuvered and outgunned the anti-imperialists. Neither the people of Cuba nor those of the Philippines were ready to join the brotherhood of nations. But whereas Cuba was already within the sphere of American influence and counted for little in the large policy being worked out in Washington, the Philippines were viewed as a vital piece in the puzzle of balance of power in the Far East. American presence there almost guaranteed a part in the China trade, a key factor in the economic and political situation in the region.

By early 1902 a constitutional government for Cuba, one modeled on that of the United States, went into effect. Not surprisingly, Cuban voters divided into two opposing political parties, Moderates and Liberals. On May 29, 1902, Estrada Tomás Palma was sworn in as the first president of the republic of Cuba. American troops were withdrawn as the Cuban ship of state was fairly launched. In anticipation of all this, Congress in Washington passed into law the Platt amendment that was, in some ways, a counterpoint to the Teller amendment. It prohibited Cuba alienating territory to any foreign power and from being politically or financially tied to any such power. Most importantly it provided for intervention by the United States, if requested, in order to maintain Cuban independence or to stabilize the government. All this was agreed to by the Cuban Constitutional Convention and became part of the law of Cuba.[17]

The inability of the Cuban electorate and its politicians to make a working proposition of representative government was soon apparent. Elections in 1905 witnessed a struggle between Moderates and Liberals that threatened to break out into civil war. By mid-August of 1906 there was open revolt by the Liberals who charged wholesale corruption of the electoral system by their opponents. It appeared that the entire edifice of republican rule was about to collapse. The Platt Amendment was intended to provide intervention by the United States if the political situation deteriorated to the breaking point. President Palma, acting through the American consul general in Havana, asked President Roosevelt to intervene by dispatching two war ships to Havana harbor. Roosevelt was most reluctant to do what he termed "a very serious thing to undertake forcible intervention" without being "absolutely certain of the equities of the case. . . ."[18] The tendency to look to Washington to solve political problems in Havana was to be avoided if at all possible. In a letter to Don Gonzala de Quesada, the Cuban Minister to the United States, Roosevelt spelled out his views further. "Our intervention in Cuban affairs will only come if Cuba shows she lacks the self-restraint necessary to secure peaceful self-government and that contending factions have plunged the country into war."[19] Nonetheless the situation worsened so that Roosevelt took a fresh and broader look at the unfolding of events.

The United States government could not be indifferent to the dangers facing American investments in the sugar industry, in both fields and factories, and this attitude tended to soften the president's position on intervention. Estimates as high as $150,000,000 in potential losses meant the administration could not remain indifferent to the apparent failure of the Cuban political system. Roosevelt consulted both the War and Navy Departments before announcing that Secretary of War Taft, accompanied by Assistant Secretary of State Robert Bacon (Elihu Root was on an extended good will tour of South America) would be the point man. Roosevelt made a careful distinction in advising Taft that his purpose was not to "intervene" in Cuban affairs but to look after American business interests. Taft, however, saw the situation for what it was, telling the president that "if we have to go in at all I am in favor of going in with as much force as we can command, so as to end the business at once."[20] He had already ascertained that a contingent of 6,000 U.S. troops was available for immediate duty. Admitting that he was unfamiliar in a detailed way with Cuban politics, Taft was not keen on taking this assignment. He had questioned the wisdom of the Teller Amendment insuring Cuba its independence almost immediately after the end of the Spanish-American War, but good soldier that he was, he was ready to be of help to his president and friend. September 19, 1906, found Taft and Bacon in Havana, having arrived on the *USS Des Moines*. Shades of February 1898? Hardly, but there was no guarantee of the outcome. There were as many as 15,000 men bearing arms and arrayed against the regime of President Palma when the American diplomatic team came ashore. Perhaps no more than a brush fire, but the flames could spread if they were not soon contained.

By whatever name, intervention/consultation/mediation, the United States was committed to "regularize" the political life of Cuba. Taft, as head of the mission, enjoyed a peculiar advantage over his chief when it came to defining American policy at the point of impact. He was on the ground, and concluded quickly that intervention it must be. Indeed, Washington had but little choice. Liberals and Moderates alike favored it when the Palma government collapsed on September 28, creating a political vacuum crying to be filled. The very next day Taft proclaimed an interim government, provisional in nature, with himself as governor. He phrased his announcement with a clear regard for Cuban sensitivities and adroitly combined it with American resolve. Accordingly, U.S. troops began to occupy the island, not to contain a revolution—fighting had never been more than a show of arms—but to "provide a background of confidence." In his extended report to the President he assured Roosevelt that the Cuban constitution had been respected, that "we are here against our will, and only for the purpose of aiding Cuba." In a sense, it boiled down to maintaining law and order, an objective that was consistent with and a common element in Taft's thinking. As he phrased it, Cuba was, for the time being, "in receivership." Especially worthy of note was Taft's address to National University of Havana. He urged his student-listeners to become men of property. They should be infused, to a goodly degree, with a spirit of mercantilism. Taft insisted at the same time that those who did accumulate wealth make a contribution to the future of their country by founding great enterprises. Their capital investments would provide employment for the many, benefiting all classes of Cuban society. Most significantly a sound economy would prove to be the foundation of a stable and secure government.[21] However optimistic Taft might sound in public discourse, he was not sanguine about the future of self-government in Cuba. As he explained to his brother Charles, Cuba's attempts at self-rule were akin to "making bricks without straw." But the Cuban crisis of 1905-06 had been resolved. The Cubans would try afresh to make republican rule a reality, under the watchful eye of the United States army.[22]

Taft's diplomatic activities in the Philippines, in Panama, and in Cuba had provided him with a learning experience of no small order, but it proved to be only the first segmented phase in what would become for him "world-ordered diplomacy." His purpose in all three of these missions had been to establish and/or to keep order, and this was to be done by a show of force, and when called for, a use of force, or to sharpen the point, a responsible use of force. Looking ahead some years, in 1915 this ex-president of the United States would be elected president of The League To Enforce Peace. As the chief spokesman of this League he no doubt drew on the lessons he had learned in his earlier days. The willful leader or the willful nation must be brought to heel in order that peace might prevail. Taft was never an advocate of brute force; rather, force worked best when combined with sympathy for if not endorsement of a party bent on war. He had had to grapple with Filipino insurrectionaries and with Cuban paramilitary squads and he had come to understand that talk alone, whether in negotiation or mediation, usually invited a veiled hint of force to move matters along in the direction of progress. There must almost always be the prospect of force, waiting in the wings, ready to come on stage at the right moment, to achieve a workable compromise. This was the instruction given him early on, the lessons of realpolitik. Such an agenda had clearly succeeded in dealing with weak nations and because he was not a martinette by nature, he inclined to call on force not as a first step but as a last resort.[23] Taft was somewhat more at ease when dealing with "lesser" nations. When it came to the new Japan, a nation commanding respect because of its political, economic, and military successes, he was to enter upon a new phase in his education as a diplomat. Japan must be dealt with, yes, but as an equal, as was established by its victory in the Sino-Japanese War of 1894, and its alliance with Great Britain from 1902, a treaty that was of the essence of balance of power as a way of keeping the peace.

The office of Secretary of War enabled Taft to have a wide view of American foreign policy. As the top official at the War Department, his position gave him stature and importance, enhancing his potential as a de facto diplomat when the opportunity might arise. Add to this President Roosevelt's wholehearted endorsement of his work. TR, of course, had an innate feel for the international affairs as they were playing out at the start of the new century, taken up as they were with alliances and treaties and ententes, any one or more of which might have implications for American policy. As a champion of the special relationship between the United States and Great Britain, beginning with London's support in the 1898 war, Roosevelt kept a keen eye on the Anglo-Japanese Treaty of 1902 (renewed in 1905). Both Britain and Japan had vital interests in the Far East, and especially in China and its trade. Outbreak of the Russo-Japanese War in 1904 put the treaty arrangements to the test and nothing was found wanting. In Roosevelt's peacemaking efforts growing out of the Russo-Japanese conflict, the President had to lean hard on the British Foreign Office to show that peace was in the best interests of both parties. In a matter of months all the nations involved were led to the conclusion that were the war to drag on, destabilization in the Far East was certain to follow. Better for all concerned—Japan and its ally (Britain) and Russia and its ally (France)—to base a future of peace on the operation of balance of power. If that could be arranged not the least of the beneficiaries would be the United States.[24]

As it happened Secretary of War Taft had planned a visit to the Philippines in the summer of 1905, having arranged to lead a congressional delegation. It was to be an opportunity for the legislators to judge the wisdom of the administration's Philippines programs in moving the islanders in the direction of a sound economy, a stable society, and a maturing polity. Roosevelt seized the day, directing Taft to stop in Tokyo. It was a matter of paying his compliments to the Japanese whom he admired as a people and a nation. But perhaps more could be achieved. Taft's visit would occur as negotiations to end the Russo-Japanese War were about to begin. The timing was exquisite as TR sought to give an indication of the good will of the American government toward Japan. To the Japanese Taft may well have seemed larger than life because of his physical appearance and his position as Secretary of War, an American samurai. In as much as Taft himself was favorably disposed toward Japan, he could be utterly sincere in what he said. But always on his mind was the question: where did the Philippines fit in Tokyo's grand strategy? Like it or not he was prepared to be blunt: hands off the Philippines.

Once in Tokyo Taft conferred with the prime minister, Taro Katsura, sending a full report of this initial contact to Secretary of State Root. The several talks between the men centered on the Philippines, Korea, and the balance of power in the Far East. Taft, who had been initially reluctant to play the role of diplomat because he felt ill-prepared, nonetheless warmed to the issues once the Philippines were discussed. Katsura stated unequivocally a disavowal of his country's hostile attitude toward the United States in possession of the Islands, and that "Japan did not harbor any oppressive designs whatsoever." He announced further that Japan, Great Britain, and the United States were the nations having a "common interest" in upholding peace in the region. In the course of their discussion Katsura dropped the other shoe. In return for Japan's regard for the United States in the Philippines, Tokyo expected to have a green light from Washington to acquire fully and finally the Korean peninsula. He spoke plainly of the absolute importance for a complete solution to the peninsula question. It was, he went on, a "logical consequence" of the Russo-Japanese War. Taft appeared to have no difficulty in agreeing with the "justice" of this position and in so doing rather daringly went out on a limb.[25] He told Katsura that the president would no doubt concur. In so saying perhaps Taft had in mind Roosevelt's verbal slap at the Koreans: "The Koreans are of the same race as the Japanese in the way that a Levantine is of the same race as Lord Milner." Upon reading Taft's account of his last meeting with Katsura, Roosevelt cabled him at once: "Your conversation with Count Katsura absolutely correct in every respect. Wish you would state to Katsura that I confirm every word you have said."[26] Japanese regard for Taft as a reliable voice of his government simply soared and worked to his advantage in 1907 on his return trip to Tokyo for another serious exchange of views regarding the Far East.

The larger meaning to grow out of the Taft-Katsura agreement was a de facto entente among Great Britain, the United States, and Japan, the raison d'être of which was maintenance of the regional status quo. Taft had read the situation rightly, if not instinctively, completely convinced that the working understanding among the three governments was how the abstract idea of balance of power was to be applied successfully in a given situation. And as he reflected on all he had seen and talked about and in an evaluation of Roosevelt's concurring judgment, he would become an advocate of balance of power as a general rule in the practice of diplomacy. All of which added to his self-confidence in the handling of diplomatic affairs, whether as Secretary of War or whatever else the future might hold for him.

Despite the tenor and texture of the Taft-Katsura understanding—a gentlemen's agreement that, not being a formal treaty, at most bound only the Roosevelt administration—friction between Tokyo and Washington remained a fact. The sources were several. Japan's disappointment in not receiving an indemnity from Russia under the terms of the Treaty of Portsmouth was seen as Roosevelt's doing; in other words, the United States, which was not a party to the treaty, should have insisted that Russia "pay up." Also, segregation of Japanese school children by the San Francisco school board was coupled with a recognition of a growing resentment at the influx of Japanese labor into the United States that competed with native-born Americans for jobs. However ill- or well-founded Tokyo's resentment was, there was little the Washington government could do to reduce the friction. And there matters remained until 1907 when the Secretary of War was again to visit the Orient. The purpose of this second trip was first of all to attend the opening of the first all-Filipino Congress. This event, long desired by Taft, was dearest to his heart, signaling as it did a crucial step in the direction of genuine self-government for the Islands. He was confident that the "experiment" in republican government was a breakthrough for the countries of East Asia. Again, Roosevelt took advantage of Taft's presence in that part of the world, asking his Secretary of War (and for Taft, Roosevelt's wish was his command) to pay another "courtesy" call on the Japanese before proceeding to Manila.

From the day of his arrival in Tokyo, September 28, until his departure, October 3, Taft was in daily conversations with the highest ranking officials of the realm, including an audience with the emperor. This latter encounter, a formality in some ways, was a reassuring sign of good relations between the two countries. The negotiations—no more than talks really—were tough affairs, with Taft on the receiving end of angry remonstrances by several members of the imperial cabinet. On the afternoon of the twenty-eighth he met with Tadasu Hayashi, the foreign minister, and the question was raised about the rumor that the United States intended to sell the Philippines. Taft was aghast at such a thought and with vehement confidence said there could be nothing further from the truth. That evening he dined at the Shipa Palace, the guest of Count Tanaka, minister to the imperial household, an official close to the emperor in all matters of public concern. Tanaka moved quickly to the issue of school segregation of Japanese children in San Francisco. He cited it as blatant racial discrimination, contrasting the treatment of oriental immigrants with that of those coming from Europe. To be sure the American envoy attempted to defuse the heated arguments presented by Tanaka in particular, insisting that there were no differences between the two peoples that could not be resolved by honorable men conducting an honorable diplomacy. And he went on to say that any thought of war was utter foolishness. But the issue would not easily go away. In the September 30 meeting Hayashi again spoke of the bitter resentment of his people that implied inequality between Japanese and Europeans in the eyes of the American government and people, underlining the discriminatory immigration policies prevailing. Taft was prepared to recognize that Japanese discontent was justified. He told Hayashi that he was in no position to promise a change of the law under the Roosevelt administration.[27]

The evening of the thirtieth Taft stole the show by delivering a reality-based but reassuring formal address to a large meeting of Japanese businessmen at the Tokyo Chamber of Commerce center. He was at his best in doing his best for American-Japanese relations. This was due in part because he totally believed in the message he was putting forth, and because his audience detected in his words that it had a friend in a high place in the Washington government and one who was very influential with the President. His focus was on the unthinkable, namely, war between the two countries, as the following passage bears out.

> War between Japan and the United States would be a crime against modern civilization. It would be as wicked as it would be insane. Neither the people of Japan nor the people of the United States desire war. The governments of the two countries would strain every point to avoid such an awful catastrophe. What has Japan to gain by it? What has the United States to gain by it? Japan has reached a point in her history when she is looking forward with confident hope to great commercial conquests. She is shaking off the effects of war and is straining every nerve for victories of peace. With the marvelous industry, intelligence and courage of her people there is nothing in trade, commerce and popular contentment and enlightenment to which she may not attain. Why should she wish a war that would stop all this?[28]

He had been fulsome in his praise of Japan and sincere in his faith in the diplomatic affinity of the nations.

Meeting with Hayashi resumed the next day, focusing once more on the immigration policy of the United States. Taft gave as a response, and somewhat as a rejoinder, that administrative rulings rather than formal treaties offered some promise of a resolution of the impasse. Another minister, no less than the premier, the Marquis Saionzi, entered the discussions. Taft described what followed as a friendly exchange of explanations of the issue, with the Marquis insisting the United States must recognize the dignity of his nation by placing such immigration rulings on an equal footing for all. Point made, but not taken, despite Taft's efforts to explain American law and practice.

By October 2 the Secretary's visit was coming to an end, a stay made the more pleasant by resuming his friendship with Count Katsura.

They agreed that peace, not war, between the two countries was the imperative to be guided by. As Katsura was no longer in the government, he spoke with limited effect from an honorable retirement, yet Taft viewed him as a kind of symbol of friendship with America.

Taft made a full report of these various conversations directly to the President. In so doing he advised Roosevelt that there was a recurring sub-text in Japan's definition of its future policy. To be specific, he concluded that the Japanese focus was to be on China. "Their attitude is centered on China, their army has been increased . . . not to fight us but because of China. They are determined to secure a predominance in Chinese affairs and to obtain every commercial concession possible and they believe it is essential to retain their armament to meet contingencies."[29] It appears that Taft did not challenge Japanese designs on China by a pointed reminder of American policy as stated in the Open Door notes. Was he playing the game of balance of power? Possibly. In any event he was moderating his rosy take on relations between the two nations. In Washington there was worry about the vulnerability of the Philippines, not only on the part of the Navy Department planners but also by the President who at one point spoke to Taft about the archipelago as "our Achilles heel."[30] Roosevelt pushed hard for the Congress to vote funds sufficient to improve the defenses of the islands and to enlarge the naval station there.

After his time in Japan Taft's next stop was Shanghai, and he was to spend some weeks in China. One of the highlights there was an address hosted by the American Association of China. It was a remarkable speech in two ways. He repeated what he had said on an earlier 1905 visit, when he had spoken to a large gathering in Canton. That is to say, he reiterated that United States policy and outlook toward China had not changed, would not change, and that the Open Door remained a central element in American thinking. Secondly, in as much as he had but recently departed from Japan, he was more conscious of Tokyo's ambitions regarding the mainland. He should be seen as giving fair warning that Chinese territorial integrity continued to be Washington's primary commitment. In his remarks the Secretary of War could not have spoken more plainly as the following excerpt demonstrates.

> The policy of the Government of the United States has been authoritatively stated to be that of seeking the permanent safety and peace of China, the preservation of Chinese territorial and administrative entity, the protection of all rights guaranteed by her to friendly Powers by treaty and international law, and, as a safeguard for the world, the principle of equal and impartial trade with all parts of the Chinese Empire. This was the policy which John Hay made famous as that of "the open door." By written memorandum, all the great Powers interested in the trade of China have subscribed to its wisdom and declared their adherence to it. The Government of the United States has not deviated in the slightest way from its attitude in this regard since the policy was announced in 1900.[31]

Beyond that Taft looked forward to the development of the Chinese empire, based on administrative and governmental reform and an increasingly valuable trade. "China for the Chinese" was much more than a slogan. For Americans Taft implied it was a heartfelt hope and expectation. All in all the Secretary was honestly positive as he described the return to China of the indemnity levied on that country in the aftermath of the Boxer Rebellion. Such an action on the part of the United States was more than "a nice sense of international obligation" that may justly increase the "friendly feelings" between the two countries.[32] Were the Chinese to develop as a great and truly sovereign state, they could rely on the United States to help maintain a balance of power in that part of the world and in the best interest of Sino-American relations.

Taft's journeying turned out to be an around the world affair. He traveled to Vladivostok where he met with Willard Straight, the United States consul at Mukden. Straight was a fierce advocate of American investment in Manchuria and eventually south of the Great Wall. Although his point of view had no immediate impact on Wall Street bankers or the government, there would come a time when Taft's advocacy of dollar diplomacy in China would owe a great deal to Straight's ideas.

From Vladivostok Taft set out for St. Petersburg aboard the Trans-Siberian railroad. It occurred to him that the Siberian plain was the Russian equivalent to the plains of the American west. If Russia were to undertake to develop this vast area, it would have much to gain domestically and in international affairs. Once in the Russian capital he met with Alexander Isvolski, the Czarist foreign minister who declared that with the decline of Russian interest in the Far East the United States should not be surprised to see the Open Door give way to Japanese dominance. Taft stayed only a few days in Russia but took the opportunity to address the American colony in St. Petersburg, in a speech that came down to little more than an appeal for good Russian-American relations. He reminded his listeners that Russia alone among the powers was sympathetic to the United States during its Civil War and again spoke somewhat romantically about the possibilities for Russian greatness should Siberia be widely settled. He also struck a personal note reminding the audience and himself that his father had been U.S. minister to the Court of Alexander III. This talk was followed the next day by a brief but friendly audience with Czar Nicholas II, another one of those courtesy calls paid absolute monarchs. It was quickly discovered the two had little to say to each other. And the Czar, taking Taft's title as Secretary of War to mean he must be interested in armies, got no response from the very civilian Taft. By this time Taft was eager to get home, going directly to Hamburg and there taking ship to the United States. During the whole of his itinerary Taft had done a solid job of promoting both the American image and American policy. This is especially true respecting Japan.[33]

In November 1908, the Root-Takahira Agreement was concluded in Washington between Secretary of State Root and the Japanese ambassador to the United States, Count Takahira. This was no more (and nothing less) than an executive understanding. It upheld the Open Door, pledged respect for each nation's possessions in the region, in short, it pledged the status quo. It is reasonable to conclude, given Taft's work in Tokyo in 1907, that his representations of the position and outlook of the United States , his insistence that peace between the two countries was vital to the interests of both, and his reassurances regarding immigration if not school segregation helped to promote Tokyo's initiatives in dealing with the State Department and its chief. Surely other factors figured in bringing about the Root-Takahira Agreement, for example, the 1908 world cruise by the Great White Fleet, the brainchild of Theodore Roosevelt. Yet at the end of the day Taft's firm and friendly dealings with the Japanese in 1905 and again 1907 greatly facilitated the 1908 rapprochement. The very next year presidential diplomacy awaited William Howard Taft, entailing responsibilities for which he was well prepared.

NOTES

[1]   Ernest May, *Imperial Democracy* (New York: Harcourt, Brace & World, 1961) presents the facts in full detail, develops the theme, and sets the tone in examining American colonialism.

[2]   A. Whitney Griswold, *The Far Eastern Policy of the United States* (New Haven: Yale University Press, 1938), pp. 75-76.

[3]   John Hay to Andrew D. White, in W.W. Malloy, *Treaties, Conventions, International Acts, Protocols, Agreements* (Washington: Government Printing Office, 1910), I, 246-47.

[4]   For a fuller appreciation of Rizal see Charles Edward Russell and E.B. Rodriguez, *The Hero of the Filipinos* (New York and London: The Century Company, 1923).

[5]   John Morgan Gates, *Schoolbooks and Krags, The United States Army in the Philippines, 1898-1902* (Westport, CT: Greenwood Press, 1973) and Stuart C. Miller, *"Benevolent Assimilation": The American Conquest of the Philippines, 1899-1903* (New Haven: Yale University Press, 1984) give full, critical accounts.

[6]   Quoted in Leon Wolff, *Little Brown Brother* (Garden City: Doubleday, 1961), p. 66.

[7]   Taft in private correspondence was bluntly realistic. E.g., Taft to John Marshall Harlan: "There is a small percentage of these people who are educated and able to exercise suffrage. The great mass of them are superstitious and ignorant and their leaders do not recognize universal suffrage." June 30, 1900, Taft Papers, reprinted in Oscar Alonso, *Theodore Roosevelt and the Philippines, 1897-1909* (Quezon City: University of the Philippines Press, 1970), p. 44. Taft to John Blair, March 16, 1905, on self-government: "certainly not for a generation and probably not for a longer time than that" will they be ready for self-rule. Ibid., p. 52.

[8]   Minger, *Taft, The Apprenticeship Years*, pp. 76-77.

[9]   Pringle, *Taft*, I, 101-03.

[10] Duffy, *Taft*, pp. 105-09.

[11] For an informal analysis of Taft and Vatican diplomacy see John T. Farrell, "Background of the Taft Mission II," *Catholic Historical Review*, 37 (April, 1951), 1-22.

[12] External Order, Roosevelt to Taft, May 9, 1904, *Letters of Theodore Roosevelt*, 8 vols, Elting E. Morison, ed. (Cambridge: Harvard University Press, 1951-54), vol. 4, pp. 787-93.

[13] Roosevelt to Taft, Oct. 18, 1904, *Letters of Roosevelt*, vol. 4, pp. 985-86.

[14] Taft to Charles Taft, Nov. 17, 1904, quoted in Minger, *Taft, The Apprenticeship Years*, p. 107.

[15] Ibid., pp. 109-10.

[16] Ibid., p. 107.

[17] For an overview of United States-Cuban relations see Harry F. Guggenheim, *The United States and Cuba: A Study in International Relations* (New York: Macmillan, 1934).

[18] Quoted in David Lockmiller, *Magoon in Cuba* (Chapel Hill: University of North Carolina Press, 1938), p. 40.

[19] Roosevelt to Taft, Sept. 14, 1906, *Letters of Roosevelt*, vol. 5, p. 412.

[20] Taft to Roosevelt, Sept. 15, 1906, Minger, *Taft, The Apprenticeship Years*, p. 124.

[21] Ibid., pp. 135-36.

[22] Ibid., p. 132.

[23] For a full treatment of the Taft-Wilson cooperation and conflict see David H. Burton, *Taft, Wilson and World Order* (Madison, NJ: Fairleigh Dickinson University Press, 2003), pp. 100-22.

[24] David H. Burton offers detail and understanding on Roosevelt's foreign adventures in *Theodore Roosevelt: Confident Imperialist* (Philadelphia: University of Pennsylvania Press, 1968).

[25] For the complete text see D.B. Goebel, *American Foreign Policy* (New York: Holt, Rinehart, and Winston, 1961), pp. 189-90.

26   Taft to Roosevelt, July 31, 1905, Minger, *Taft, The Apprenticeship Years*, p. 148.

27   Minger provides a detailed account, ibid., pp. 152-57.

28   Taft, "Japan and Her Relations with the United States," *The Collected Works of William Howard Taft*, David H. Burton, ed. (Athens, OH: Ohio University Press, 2001), I, 115-19.

29   Taft to Roosevelt, Oct. 18, 1907, Minger, *Taft, The Apprenticeship Years*, p. 161.

30   Roosevelt to Taft, Aug. 21, 1907, *Letters of Roosevelt*, vol. 5, p. 772.

31   Taft, "Japan and Her Relations with the United States," *Works*, I, 106-14.

32   Ibid.

33   Pringle, *Taft*, I, 332-33.

3 . EVOLVING VISION

The world appeared to be at peace in March 1909, as Taft assumed the power and the responsibility of the presidency of the United States. If the surface of international politics was smooth, underneath there were troubling signs of impending conflict between and among the Powers. Great Britain, France, and Russia were members of the Triple Entente, a coming together of sometime rivals now bonded by fear of the ambitions of the German Empire in the hands of a headstrong ruler, Kaiser Wilhelm II. In her own interests Germany had helped to form the Triple Alliance, bringing the Austro-Hungarian Empire and the Kingdom of Italy to her side. Japan, to be sure, remained an ally of Great Britain. The United States was committed to neither of the competing alliances. It was, nonetheless, more historically and contemporaneously friendly to the Entente nations. And then there was the "special relationship" with Britain, which at the very least signaled acceptance of the status quo. The resulting problem: the stability of the status quo with the Anglo-French defending themselves at home and in their empires, and the Germans eager to build an empire of their own at the expense of Britain and/or France if need be. The United States hardly figured in this interaction of rival alliances, content to mind the affairs of the Americas, and always sensitive to the pretensions of the Monroe Doctrine. True, Washington looked protectively on the Philippines, secure in the belief that London and Tokyo were of one mind when it came to power politics in the Far East. Given his considerable experience in the shaping of American foreign policy it is not surprising President Taft was prepared to promote friendly relations with both Japan and the New China, as at the same time he believed, and was ready to act upon his conviction, that the United States must help with the economic problems of Central American nations looking to stabilize politically that area of the American hemisphere.

The unifying theme in all these diplomatic initiatives is international cooperation leading on to a mutual respect for the nations involved. In other words, this was to be the beginning of a world-ordered diplomacy that would evolve naturally, leading eventually to an international organization whose purpose would be peace within the community of nations. In keeping with the tenets of anthropological evolution, this world order would not be accomplished without struggle. Just as social Darwinism was superseded intellectually by pragmatism, so Taft's foreign policy steps went in the direction of an agenda that implied a well-thought-out series of diplomatic adjustments.

The question may well be asked about why there was no strong evidence of the influence of Sumner's preachments of Social Darwinism on Taft's public positions and policies. If anything, he was pragmatic in his approach to seeking resolution of the problems that faced the nation. He was not a pragmatist, however, and not given to abstractions or faithful to this or that school of thought. There was, rather, a practicality in his way of thinking and doing. Subconsciously perhaps he believed in the workability of congressional law and court reform, provided they conformed to the Constitution. As an American he could only wonder in admiration at the success of a federal government that, despite the Civil War breakdown, demonstrated its ultimate workability with the reconstruction of the union. It would not be natural, however, to associate him in theory with either Charles S.S. Pierce or William James, just as it would be wrongheaded to treat Herbert Spencer or William Graham Sumner as a presence in the mind or in action. And despite his lack of Christian orthodoxy, William Howard Taft was a traditionalist in keeping with the historic values of the American people to which he was altogether faithful. He was alert to the place and uses of these values well before he went out to the Philippines where he first came to appreciate the dynamics of mind over matter in world affairs. Similarly, in domestic politics his mind and spirit were sympathetic to reform.

He was, after all, a conservative progressive, after the manner of Theodore Roosevelt when TR was in the White House.

As closely tied to Theodore Roosevelt in his foreign policy experience as Taft had been, he preferred his own methods of proceeding. His record in office, irrespective of success or failure, would be distinctively his own in character. While pursuing his course of action, the President appeared far less eager to convince the country (and himself) that he was not Roosevelt's clone than had been the case in domestic matters. He was well-equipped to design and, he hoped, to carry out a foreign policy in which trade and investments ("dollar diplomacy" as it was called) had a determining role. Unlike Roosevelt, Taft did not despise the "economic man," but understood him and sympathized with his aims. He was determined to be guided by the force of trade and not the force of arms in his dealings with other nation states.

To carry such a policy forward, the President proposed to make use of a Department of State that was to be reorganized to meet the demands of a new foreign policy process in a new era. Philander C. Knox was appointed Secretary of State and he, in turn, selected Francis M. Huntington-Wilson to be his First Assistant Secretary. It is to the latter official that much of the credit must be given for conceptualizing how the Department was now to function. Geopolitical divisions were established for Western Europe, Latin America, the Far East, and the Near East. Staffing came from experts in the Foreign Service who had gained experience in these areas of the world. A Division of Information was created for the purpose of keeping all diplomatic posts abreast of current foreign policy. At the same time the Bureau of Trade Relations was expanded. Two new senior posts, those of Counselor and Resident Diplomat, were also brought into being. Also critical to the new look was a chief-of-staff system in which the First Assistant (Huntington-Wilson) would coordinate all information and consult on policy by means of direct and consistent access to the Secretary himself.

President Taft was greatly pleased with these arrangements because to him they meant that policy could now be more efficiently administered, and therefore America's national interests among the powers would be better served. The President had what can only be described as a "touching faith" in the efficiency of an administrative mechanism.

Because Taft set so much store on the new organization it is necessary to consider briefly the men who were now expected to make the Department machinery (and thereby the foreign policy of the United States which was its raison d'être) run smoothly. Secretary Knox was a lawyer, with a lawyer's way in government. The State Department was his client and in any international disagreement it was his duty, as it had been his courtroom responsibility, to win his case. Yet diplomacy is often a matter of tact and conciliation rather than judgments rendered for plaintiff or defendant, something that Knox was not able to appreciate. Purposeful about his work, he was too often inclined to see the Department apart from the government overall. For example, though a onetime United States senator, he made little effort to take senators' advice before seeking the Senate's consent. His relations with the press were even more negative, verging on hostility. Though one of the crucial areas of President Taft's diplomacy was to be Central America, Knox had a positive disdain for Latin Americans in his dealings with individual diplomats. According to Mitchell Innes of the British Embassy, Secretary Knox was "too much the lawyer and too little a student of man."[1]

The second in command was Huntington-Wilson, scion of a wealthy Chicago family. He was drawn to public service after the fashion of an aristocrat. Huntington-Wilson began his diplomatic career by spending nine years as second secretary of the legation in Tokyo, where he gained considerable knowledge of the Far East. By 1906 he was back in Washington as assistant secretary under Elihu Root. A third figure of note in the State Department was Alvey A. Adee who had started as a

junior embassy officer in Madrid in 1869. From 1877 to 1924 he was
with the Department in Washington, and during Taft's presidency
served as third assistant secretary. His age and experience made him
very knowledgeable, but not always in agreement on United States policy from 1909 to 1913.

Before undertaking an issue-by-issue consideration of foreign affairs
under Taft, it may be useful to identify the large objectives that the
President set for himself and his administration. It is not too much to
claim that under Taft the business of American diplomacy was business.
As early as 1908 in an address to the Commercial Club in Chicago, the
future President talked of the "opportunity for vast expansion in the
sale of our manufactured goods in the Orient, in Japan, in China, and
the Philippines, and even as far as India."[2] The question that he then
raised for his business audience was whether the United States was
going to take advantage of the opportunities that its manufacturing
capacity virtually necessitated. Taft was not thinking, he said, of today
or tomorrow but of a half century hence. Expressing similar thoughts
regarding the Caribbean, Secretary Knox urged in 1910 that true stability was best established not by military but by economic and social
forces, and that financial stability contributed perhaps more than any
other one factor to political stability.[3]

The evidence points in the direction of a post-Rooseveltian foreign
policy in its method of operation. The government, by recourse to
diplomacy, ought to stabilize two of the more uneasy areas of the world,
the Orient and the Caribbean, as a way of enabling American financial
and commercial interests to obtain an ever-increasing share of economic development there. In such undertakings, the President recognized
that the United States was in a very real competition with other
advanced industrial countries. It was just such rivalry, in fact, that left
the United States with little choice but to act. More specifically, the
objective of American policy in the Caribbean was to dominate the area

commercially and to shore it up politically, if possible, to the exclusion of other nations. In the Far East the United States sought to persuade other nations to accommodate themselves to an Open Door in China. Stability, commerce, and economic opportunities constituted the triad of Taft's foreign policy objectives.

At the same time as the President thought to impart a soft touch to the hard facts of realpolitik by stressing economic rather than political purpose, he pursued other diplomatic objectives that were particular personal favorites. Taft very much wanted to negotiate a reciprocal trade treaty with Canada that he was convinced would benefit both countries. And he was fervent in his desire to establish treaties of arbitration with Great Britain and France as an example to other nations to prefer peaceful over warlike solutions to international disputes. This latter aim marked a sharp break with the foreign policy of Roosevelt. Taft's failure to achieve either of these treaties was a source of genuine disappointment. However, with 1914 looming on the horizon, it must be said that in the matter of international peace the American President was swimming against a disastrously strong tide.

Several American Presidents in the early twentieth century looked fondly on the Caribbean Basin as a variation of mare nostrum that implied both opportunities and responsibilities for the nation. Taft was no exception. Such an attitude was both understandable, given the geography, and necessary, because of the political unreliability of some of the countries involved. In December 1908 the President-elect wrote: "I expect to continue the same policy toward Latin America thus so [sic] happily entered on by Mr. Root and Mr. Roosevelt." In the same statement he went on to tell John Barrett, who was director of the Internal Bureau of American Republics, that he would "count my administration fortunate if further steps can be taken and new measures adopted to secure closer and mutually more beneficial commercial associations. . . ." Taft proposed to build on the earlier accomplishments by

developing a business relationship that would be at once more sophis-
ticated and more lasting than the political remedies offered, for
example, in Cuba by Roosevelt. By peaceful and profitable trade he
hoped to siphon off some of the ill will that TR's actions in Panama and
the Dominican Republic had engendered.[4]

The Roosevelt legacy for the Caribbean was a mixed one. The Big
Stick had certainly controlled events in Panama that led to that tiny
province's revolt against the Colombian government at Bogota and was
directly responsible for the speedy diplomatic recognition extended to
the dubious republic. In contrast, Roosevelt had drawn no sword in
1904 when the Dominican Republic sought protection by the United
States from its European creditors. Instead of Marines, the President
dispatched civil servants to supervise the operation of the customs
houses there. This maneuver had more than a measure of success in
meeting the immediate problem of sparing the Dominicans a European
naval bombardment or troop landing, either of which would have constituted a violation of the Monroe Doctrine. But two questions
remained. What were the long-term prospects for stable government in
the Dominican nation? And were President Roosevelt's actions legal?
The United States Senate steadfastly refused to approve the
Dillingham-Sanchez Protocol of 1905, providing for Americans as tax
collectors. After consulting his advisors, including Taft, who observed
good-naturedly that they had agreed to surrender "to the usurpation of
the executive," Roosevelt continued the protocol in effect while his
opponents fumed.

The seeds of dollar diplomacy had been sown in the handling of the
Dominican fiscal crisis of 1904, with the support of Taft; he, however,
would be much more respectful of constitutional proprieties when it
came his turn to pacify the Caribbean. What Roosevelt had done was,
nevertheless, a model for American policy under Taft, to a large degree
because it was judged to have worked. According to Secretary Knox,

the undertakings of the United States in the Dominican Republic had been nothing short of "brilliant," so what had succeeded there might be made to work elsewhere should the opportunity arise.

From the outset of American involvement in the Caribbean, mare nostrum threatened to become a Serbonian bog. The utter inability of many of the nations in the area to maintain their political equilibrium was a constant factor that American diplomats had to deal with. Taft once expressed his frustration by telling Knox that he wished he had the right to "knock their [governments'] heads together until they should maintain peace between them."[5] Perhaps such measures would not be required after all. In 1907, with the good offices of Mexico and the United States, five Central American nations—Costa Rica, Salvador, Guatemala, Honduras, and Nicaragua—signed the Washington Convention. To remain in effect for ten years, it was intended as a treaty of peace and friendship among the signatory countries. Part of its purpose was to discourage revolutions by denying any recognition of governments that came to power by extralegal methods. The effectiveness of this convention was problematical. Should it break down, the result could require the Taft administration to make some application of the Roosevelt Corollary to the Monroe Doctrine.

During the years 1909 to 1913, Nicaragua was the primary United States worry. President José Zelaya was particularly troublesome in Washington's view because he appeared to have his eye on Salvadorian territory. In addition he threatened from time to time to rescind commercial concessions enjoyed by Americans and other foreigners. His unpredictability in such matters tended to make United States diplomacy wary. When, in the fall of 1909, a revolt broke out against Zelaya, the Taft administration was prepared to take advantage of this development by looking kindly on the rebel leader, Juan Estrada. Should he become President, Estrada would be more amenable to American plans to dominate Central America.

Washington sought to keep a strict neutrality in the matter, following the advice of Alvey Adee, but diplomats in the field openly favored Estrada. American public opinion was momentarily antagonized when two United States citizens serving with the rebel forces were captured and executed. The mini-civil war itself might have been a pretext for Roosevelt to threaten to use troops. Taft's State Department, at the suggestion of Huntington-Wilson, was aggressive enough to consider the seizure of Managua, and to hold it until such time as a good government was formed. Actually, the administration decided against unilateral intervention but severed diplomatic relations on December 1. Great Britain expressed satisfaction with what was termed the "hard-Knox policy" of the Americans. Mexico, which had been cosponsor of the Washington Convention, remained opposed to any overt action that might be construed as anti-Zelayan. Public opinion in the United States had cooled at the same time. Taft continued, nonetheless, to look for some means literally to compel peace among the Central American States. He judged the moral suasion that Mexico preferred to be insufficient.

To complicate matters for the State Department, Estrada, the American favorite, encountered stiff opposition in his efforts to win control of the country. Zelaya had given way to José Madriz, who had been elected President according to law, and Madriz had gained some following. American encouragement of Estrada finally carried the day, but only after months of confusion. With the Dominican model in mind, the Taft people insisted that in return for diplomatic recognition, the new regime seek a loan, to be guaranteed by American supervision of Nicaraguan customs. Once the United States had a firm hold on this main source of public revenue, it could pretty well dictate the politics of the country, including provisions in the constitution, elections, and policy, whether domestic or foreign. Estrada agreed to these American stipulations.

Dollar diplomacy in this instance was only halfway home. Estrada showed himself to be a weak ruler and was soon succeeded by Adolfo Diaz. Opposition to this latter administration quickly surfaced, led by Luis Mena, Minister of War. Another American worry was that a majority of Nicaraguans was against the American-approved government and resented interference in their affairs. Finally, the Senate of the United States was a very high hurdle for the Taft administration to clear. There was no prospect that the President would ignore the upper house and resort to executive agreement. Roosevelt's behavior in the Dominican affair held no allure for Taft. Instead, he mounted what for him was a maximum effort to win senatorial approval of Nicaragua's status as a client state. He delivered a special message to Congress, contacted individual senators, and argued repeatedly that a Nicaragua stabilized by American dollars was vital to the safety of the Panama Canal, then coming to completion. But the Senate rejected Taft's Nicaraguan gamble in 1911.

In Nicaragua, meanwhile, Diaz's regime grew shaky. Luis Mena made his bid for power in July 1912. The United States requested assurances from President Diaz that the government could and would protect American-owned property. Such assurances were not forthcoming. The next month American sailors and marines, upwards of 2,000 troops eventually, came ashore. Huntington-Wilson drew up a set of recommendations for the President to consider, in which he urged intervention for an extended period. "We think if the United States does its duty promptly and thoroughly and impressively in Nicaragua, it would strengthen our hand and lighten our task . . . throughout Central America and the Caribbean and would even have some effect on Mexico."[6] Taft accepted these recommendations, and American troops stayed to restore orderly government, eliminate the Zelayan-Mena elements, and protect American business interests. This excursion into dollar diplomacy made a turn that was certainly not planned and probably not wanted. Whatever the case, President Taft offered no apology for what had taken place.

Much the same judgment must be made relative to dollar diplomacy in Honduras, though details might vary from country to country. That small nation was in debt in the amount of $110 million, mostly owed to English bond holders. Under considerable pressure from London, the Honduran President, Miguel Davila, had agreed to pay off the British portion of this debt by means of forty annual installments. The State Department termed this plan inimical to the best interests of the United States. With such large sums of money leaving the country, there would be little chance that other foreign creditors, including Americans, would be repaid. Adee and Huntington-Wilson put forward a proposal to involve the United States in Honduran affairs by placing Americans in charge of the customs houses. J.P. Morgan and Company was contracted for the purpose of arranging a loan to Honduras, in return for which the government would meet American terms for control. In effect, the United States was to guarantee the loan in pursuit of political stability for that small nation. Conditions in Honduras were unsettled and the American bankers grew edgy, but the ultimate reason for the collapse of the scheme was the refusal of the American Senate to endorse the State Department proposals.[7]

In both Nicaragua and Honduras, the model that the Taft administration attempted to imitate—but always within the letter of the Constitution—had been laid down in the Dominican Republic some years before. Events were soon to demonstrate that it was a questionable model, after all. Within five years of American withdrawal in 1912, the country was again on the threshold of financial ruin. President Ramon Caceres, who had come to power in 1905, had been a positive influence. He was both strong and popular. Upon his assassination in 1911 he was succeeded by General Elalio Victoria, a weak and foolish man. The effect of his tenure in office was a predictable destabilization.

The situation quickly grew serious enough to move W.W. Russell, the American minister, to urge some form of intervention. In Washington, Huntington-Wilson prepared an elaborate memorandum that called for the removal of Victoria and amnesty for his political enemies who had gone into hiding. Meantime the Navy stood ready, underscoring the seriousness of American concern. During a meeting at the White House, the State Department plan was adopted, at least in general outline. What followed was intervention in the affairs of the Dominican Republic reminiscent of actions taken by the Roosevelt administration. But there was a constitutional difference. No protocol was signed that might require senatorial approval. Under the direction of Russell and two assistant commissioners, new officials were allowed to take over the running of the government. A loan from National City Bank of New York in the sum of $500,000 was arranged to enable the new Dominican administration to settle in. There were few political or constitutional complaints in the United States compared to the lashing Roosevelt had taken. Strictly speaking, all the Taft administration had done was to approve the loan by the New York bank. Neither treaty nor executive agreement was required.[8]

President Taft had full knowledge of the various efforts to seek ascendancy in Latin America by means of dollar diplomacy, and he gave them his endorsement. Often the particular initiatives out of which larger policy emerged came from high-ranking State Department officials who persuaded the President to move ahead. The influence of Knox, Huntington-Wilson, and Adee was manifest. In contrast, when neighboring Mexico underwent internal upheavals that promised to lead to a Mexican Revolution, Taft was the mainstay of an American neutrality policy about which some of his advisors were dubious. He understood the nature of the revolution better than did Secretary Knox, and he was determined to exercise firm control of United States diplomacy toward Mexico. As for diplomacy's logical extension, war, Taft had set his face against American military intervention. His advocacy of neutrality was, nonetheless, a mixture of conciliation and force, whereby the administration demonstrated its genuine concern for the lives of the 40,000 Americans residing in Mexico; yet it was careful to avoid offending Mexico's sensitivity about possible intrusion into its domestic affairs.

The historic anti-Americanism of Mexico was aggravated in the first years of the twentieth century by heavy United States investments that had doubled between 1900 and 1914. This increase had brought the total dollar-stake in the developing Mexican economy to hundreds of millions. Americans were perceived as foreign landlords by many Mexican nationalists, and with good reason, since they controlled an estimated forty percent of the country's property while Mexicans owned less than thirty-five percent. President Porfirio Diaz had made substantial concessions to outside investors in order to bring the nation's economy out of its long slumber and into the modern century. His very success in this endeavor supplied political enemies with an explosive issue: foreign landlordism. By the time President Taft had come into office, Mexico was growing increasingly restive under Diaz, who ruled the country with ruthless efficiency. A new Mexican leader appeared in the person of the young idealist Francisco Madero. Madero defiantly attacked the Diaz willingness to subsist on the crusts of foreign investments. He also constituted a threat to the security of American dollars in Mexico. Before long there was a sputter of revolutionary activity, made the more ominous for the United States by the revolutionaries' easy access to arms and supplies from across the border.

Taft was vitally interested in Mexican affairs from the start of his administration. He not only visited the aged Diaz on the border, signaling his friendship, but also transferred Henry Lane Wilson from his post in Brussels to Mexico City to be his special eyes and ears. Wilson was an experienced diplomat who had served in Chile, spoke Spanish, and had some appreciation of the Latin American temperament. He was also sympathetic with the American practice of investing in Mexico's underdeveloped economy. As Taft remarked, "we have two billions of American capital in Mexico that will be greatly endangered if Diaz were to die and his government go to pieces." Such a statement was but a variation of the dollar diplomacy mentality that Taft had displayed in Nicaragua and elsewhere: the protection of dollars already in place and earning income. The President was apprehensive, confiding to his wife that he hoped Diaz's demise would not come until he himself had left the Presidency.[9]

Ambassador Wilson, once on site, detected serious troubles immediately ahead. He made a special trip to Washington in March 1911 to report his assessment to the President. The crisis was deepening and the lid might blow off at any time. Alarmed by this news, Taft acted quickly to protect American interests. He ordered a rapid mobilization of 20,000 troops along the United States-Mexican border and placed American naval units on alert in the Gulf of Mexico. "It seems to me my duty was clear," as he explained his moves. "Under all circumstances it was quite within my province as Commander-in-Chief to order the army out for maneuvers; so I put that face upon it. . . . Simultaneously I took care to assure the Mexican authorities that the move had no significance which could be tortured into hostility to the government of Mexico."[10] President Taft was clearly in charge of policy toward Mexico during the first years of the revolution.

The mobilization order made it imperative to mute even an implication that the nation was about to intervene in the domestic troubles of its neighbor across the border. As Taft told Archie Butt, he was going "to sit tight on the lid, and it will take a great deal to pry me off."[11] This determination he shared with the country by making public a letter he had sent to General Leonard Wood, Army Chief of Staff, shortly after the troop call-up. The President was especially intent on making the constitutional argument about intervention. Only with congressional approval, he told Wood, was intervention even to be contemplated; approval he was sure would not be forthcoming. Taft had been able to take an unassailable position. To those who feared a recrudescence of Big Stick diplomacy, he had but to reaffirm his deference to the will of Congress. To those who favored intervention (for whatever reason), he had but to reiterate that the authority lay with the legislature in the war-making process. Yet the mobilization order demonstrated forcefully that the United States was maintaining a careful watch on events in Mexico.

Unfortunately, once unleashed, the dogs of revolution are not easy to curb. Diaz retired from office in May 1911, and was succeeded by Madero, who was unable to pull the country together; by February 1913 he gave way to Victoriana Huerta. Madero was executed shortly thereafter. Mexico reeled under the impact of repeated blows. The state of Coahuila proclaimed its independence as anarchy threatened to engulf the land. American investments were increasingly at risk. To the public, Taft continued to show the face of restraint, despite cries from the oil lobby, congressmen from the Southwest, and even Theodore Roosevelt, who faulted him for lack of leadership. Privately the President took the position that he "must protect our people in Mexico as far as possible, and their property by having the [Mexican] Gov't understand there is a God of Israel and he is on duty."[12] To his great relief, his term of office came to an end just before the Mexican Revolution entered a new and uglier phase. But so long as he was Commander-in-Chief, William Howard Taft had kept the peace.

The second major area of foreign policy concern for the Taft administration was the Far East. China was the centerpiece of what A.T. Mahan had written about in *The Problem of Asia*, and it often preoccupied both the President and the State Department. According to Philander Knox, it was a common saying that "China took all the time of the Department, and the rest of the world received what was left over." For all of that, President Taft did not appear to be any more consistently involved in China than in Latin American matters, though his input was often more eye-catching. When he came into office in 1909, he immediately set about addressing the problem of China, which for American planners was the problem of the Open Door.

Taft's Far Eastern policy was based largely on a belief in the efficacy of dollar diplomacy. In this sense, the main elements of his administration's foreign policy were of one piece, a set of moves to be made in Asia and in Latin America, hoping for good effects for American business. Where American business was ascendant, its political influence was sure to be strong. There were two basic reasons why Taft advocated dollar diplomacy, each of which illuminates his public philosophy. He deemed it a peaceful variant of imperialist expansion that in the long run would materially benefit the lives of people in backward parts of the world. Both peace and material improvement were important objectives in Taft's total outlook. Secondly, the benefits that presumably would accrue to numerous American business enterprises had to appeal to the President's conviction that capitalism—which had achieved its fullest and most prosperous expression in the United States—would be strengthened. In his own mind, especially with regard to China, Taft saw himself building upon foundations laid down in previous years.

To accomplish the transition to a modern state, China required both monetary and technical assistance in amounts that only some combination of the advanced industrial states could fully supply. President Taft believed it was time for the United States to become involved in the process. Just as he was coming into office, China was completing negotiations for a large foreign loan to make possible extensive railroad expansion—the so-called Hukuang Loan. An American group that included J.P. Morgan Company, National City Bank, Kuhn, Loeb and

Company, and First National Bank was hastily organized, with the purpose of attempting forced entry into the already established European bank consortium. While the State Department advised the American Group of the opportunity and urged the various investment houses to participate, Taft took more direct action. He made an appeal to Prince Chun, the Prince Regent: "I have an intense personal interest in making use of American capital in the development of China, and an increase in her material prosperity without entanglements or creating embarrassments affecting the growth of her independent political powers and the preservation of her territorial integrity."[13] When China bowed to presidential pressure so forcefully stated, dollar diplomacy offered promise of a bright future in the Orient. It was, in essence, Taft's version of the Big Stick, according to Willard Straight, who was himself busy advising the American Group.

Secretary Knox was soon preparing follow-up moves to Taft's bold assertions. He drew up a plan to neutralize Manchuria, which at the time was coming more and more under the sway of Japan and Russia as a result of their hold on the Manchurian railroads. The American proposal was that all railroads in Manchuria be organized into a single system that China would own but that the powers would jointly operate. Furthermore, American capital would be offered to construct a new line from Chinchow to Aigun that would flesh out the system and compete with the South Manchurian line administered at the time by the Japanese, if the proposed joint venture failed to be accepted. In any event the preferred status of Japan and Russia would be diminished. And, since the United States would be guaranteed some place in the growth of Manchuria, the Open Door would be maintained. While the scheme was that of Secretary Knox, the President had given it his careful consideration and approval, no doubt in part because American bankers were ready to act. Neither Japan nor Russia was prepared to turn over roads they controlled, and, in fact, they cooperated to scotch

Knox's grand design. Since Taft was a dollar diplomat and no more—having no intention of forcing the consortium under a threat of war—the Knox plan died aborning, despite the President's efforts to keep it alive in the thinking of the American financiers.

So intent was the Taft administration on gaining political recognition of Chinese affairs by means of fiscal support and cooperation that Knox next proceeded to the question of the pending Chinese Currency Loan. As part of the modernization process, China was seeking loans from various countries, including the United States, to underwrite its money system. A group of American investors was more than willing to provide the Chinese with what they required, on condition that they employ an American as their key advisor. This demand greatly complicated the negotiations because the competing European lenders were deeply suspicious of the intention of the United States and worked to thwart the plans of the State Department. Taft expressed himself firmly on the necessity of the American appointment, instructing Knox to "insist on naming the advisor . . . we do not propose to give up the advantage inherent under the circumstances."[14] (The President, furthermore, told the special Chinese envoy, Lian Tun-yen, who was in Washington at the time, much the same thing.) The conclusion of the loan negotiations came in April 1911, but only after Taft and Knox had withdrawn their demands respecting the advisor. Meanwhile, American exports to China actually declined. Valued at $58 million in 1905, by 1910 the total exports amounted to no more than $16 million. By any estimate, the immediate results of dollar diplomacy were disappointing.

Whether enough time remained to redress the faltering balance of power in Asia could well depend on the outcome of the Chinese Revolution of 1911. In December of that year Dr. Sun Yat-sen became President of the Republic of China, as the Manchu dynasty faded into the past. Taft seemed willing to recognize the new government, for whatever benefit such a unilaterial action might have for the United

States, though he made no formal move. In this matter, he trailed public opinion, which was calling for full recognition. In his annual message
to Congress in December 1912, the President continued to delay any
official announcement pending the emergence of a clearly stable and
reliable regime. The matter was not resolved when Taft left office.[15]

For Taft, diplomacy that took into account the economic fortunes
and misfortunes of countries was a matter of enlightened rather than
self-serving policy. With reference to a reciprocity treaty with Canada
this was especially the case. He viewed trade between his country and
its northern neighbor as a natural outgrowth of proximity, common language and culture, and peoples governed by law, not by men. From
another angle the President's submission of a free trade proposal to
Congress in January 1911 was an effort to revive the principle of the
Elgin-Marcy Treaty of 1854. Granted the commercial landscape had
altered considerably since the mid-nineteenth century, yet some of
these very changes encouraged Taft to try to bring the two nations
together as congenial trading partners. This is not to argue that he
indulged in the fanciful prospect of the United States and Canada in
some kind of a North American *Zollverein* leading on to a common
nation. Opponents from both sides of the border often advertised this
as the ultimate outcome of free trade but they did so to embarrass Taft
and to frighten voters. If anything, the President was realistic about
such a turn of events, describing it as both unlikely and undesirable.

What were the particular pros and cons from the American and the
Canadian sides? The United States could expect to tap into the market
for manufactures in Canada to a significant degree. It would gain access
to raw materials and it was likely to lessen the cost of foodstuff for the
American consumer. For that very reason farmers south of the border
feared the competition of Canadian wheat, and workers worried about
depressed wages and a loss of jobs. New England fishermen in particular resisted the free entry of foreign fish into the market. Looked at

from the Canadian perspective, the country could expect greater sales of farm products and reduced prices for manufactured goods. However, opponents of reciprocity pointed out that trade would be from north to south pulling the nations together and weakening east-west trade that worked to bind the far western provinces to central and eastern Canada. Furthermore, increasingly heavy investments from American banks and companies would lead to greater and greater foreign ownership. Of course all such arguments pro and con were part of public and political discourse, but it would remain for the legislative processes in Washington and Ottawa to make the final determination. Taft found it too easy to dismiss opposition arguments as petty, short-range worries, considering himself as having the wiser, long-range view. So convinced was he that he was willing to take the risk while admitting that a treaty of reciprocity could "blow me out of the water politically but I think ultimately there will come a realization that it will help this country."[16]

As early as November 1910 Taft had directed Secretary of State Knox to consult with W.S. Fielding, the Canadian Minister of Finance, with a view to smoothing the path toward free trade. After further discussions in Washington a decision was reached whereby under the Payne-Aldrich Tariff minimum rates would apply to all trade with Canada, looking to a new, comprehensive arrangement. Earl Grey, the Governor General of Canada, endorsed the hoped-for understanding along with Sir Wilfred Laurier, the Liberal premier, and Lord Bryce, His Majesty's ambassador to the United States. In January 1911 Knox was in regular conversations with Canadian officials ironing out details of a "legislative agreement." The American position was to have both houses of Congress vote for the agreement, thereby avoiding recourse to the Senate's rule whereby a two-thirds majority was needed for approval if the "legislative agreement" were given treaty form. Taft sent a special message to the Senate asking for approval. The President, in fact, mounted an offensive, telling one senator, William

Bradley of Kentucky, that "I regard this as the most important measure of my administration" in soliciting his vote of support.[17] Indeed, he campaigned widely in the West, seeking to pressure Congress.

As it developed Taft was in the fight of his life. Some legislators resented his "coercion" by spoken and written word; others believed that his preoccupation with this one piece of legislation was leading to a loss of focus. Since the proposal came in the form of a revenue bill it originated in the House of Representatives where it passed easily. The vote was 221 to 92. A majority of Democrats joined fewer Republicans. But the Senate did not act before adjournment, which prompted the President to call a special session of Congress in early April. The upper house voted its support as well.

Canadian reciprocity has been termed the President's "most significant legislative victory of the Sixty-second Congress, and possibly of his whole presidency."[18] But meanwhile the fight over the law spilled into the streets of public and political discourse. Speaker of the House Champ Clark proclaimed this agreement as a means of bringing Canada—"every square foot of British North America"—under the control of the United States.[19] Theodore Roosevelt weighed in with the remark that the political effects of free trade "would make Canada an adjunct of the United States."[20] These highly publicized observations may have been made with good intentions, but this truculent American attitude made many Canadians wary about their nation's future. By mid-summer the "legislative arrangement" was in place in so far as the United States was concerned, and President Taft had reason to be pleased with the outcome. But Canada had yet to be heard from.

The Canadian parliamentary elections were held in September of that year. Very largely they were fought out over acceptance or rejection of the American proposal. Laurier's party favored it, arguing it should be judged on its commercial merits. But the Conservatives urged voters to see the short- and long-range political implications.

In so saying they were able to quote copiously from a number of American law makers. The Conservatives won control of parliament and rejected the American offer. The new premier, Robert Borden, referred to the president as "tricky Taft," which gives some idea how troubled was the electorate by the careless pronouncements of certain American politicians. In Taft's own words, the results of the Canadian decision "hit him between the eyes."

Taft's efforts at commercial conciliation, nonetheless, underline the direction of his foreign policy thinking, one that had evolved from the dollar diplomacy appropriate to Central American countries to free trading with the mature ecopolity of Canada. Through trade carried out amicably rather than fiercely, peoples and nations could come together. By interacting positively and thereby improving their economies, better political relations between trading partners would follow. Taft was convinced that a world-ordered economy would facilitate if not guarantee a world-ordered international community. As each of the steps along the way was taken, it would be guided by the lamp of enlightened diplomacy.

That the President was increasingly preoccupied with peace among the leading nations is borne out clearly by his proposal to seek arbitration treaties with Great Britain and France.[21] Arbitration, as an abstraction and, perhaps, as a proposal of limited application, had been bruited about almost from the time of the First Hague Conference in 1899. But participation by the United States had been consistently opposed by the Senate's negative stance that had completely undermined the several arbitration proposals it had considered before Taft came into office. Well aware of this, the President, at a meeting of the Connecticut State Fair in September, 1911, came directly to the point.

> Personally, I don't see any more why matters of national honor should not be referred to a court of arbitration any more than matters of property or national proprietorship. . . . I don't see why questions of honor may not be submitted

to a tribunal supposed to be composed of men of honor, to
abide by their decisions as well as any other question of differences arising between nations.[22]

Taft could not have been more blunt in expressing his views, or
more at odds with the mind of the Senate should he attempt to have
such a treaty passed into law. Some months later the President told
Archie Butt that a genuine arbitration treaty "will be the great jewel of
my administration. But just as it will be the greatest act during these
four years it will also be the greatest failure if I do not get it ratified."[23]
Taft had forthrightly identified himself with the concept and the practice of international arbitration. His statement was the equivalent of
"here I take my stand, I can not do otherwise." It is interesting to note
that in communicating with his confidante, Archie Butt, he explained
his March 1910 announcement in the following way: "I had no definite
policy in mind . . . I was inclined merely to offset opposition to the four
battleships for which I was fighting and I threw that suggestion out
merely to neutralize the sting of old Carnegie and other peace cranks."[24]
If this was in fact a tactical maneuver to promote his naval program it
should be pointed out that Taft was thinking of peace and force as coor-
dinates. In other words, peace would depend on the willingness and
the ability of the leading nations to make use of armies and navies to
maintain international law and order. In so arguing Taft was speaking
subconsciously in terms he would utter altogether deliberately when,
less than five years later, he would be the chief spokesman of the
League To Enforce Peace. As in the Philippines, he had called on the
army to keep peace so that responsible government might evolve for
the Island people. This proposition, force needed to bring about peace,
he was tending to invoke as a general rule.

Early in 1911 Taft and Secretary of State Knox went to work to ham-
mer out the language the arbitration treaties would require to render
them meaningful and acceptable to the signatory nations. Both Lord

Bryce and the French ambassador, Jules Jusserand, were encouraging by word and by deed. Taft was determined the language would read that the parties agreed to submit to arbitration all "justiciable" issues without reference to the Senate's role in the treaty-making process. On August 3, 1911, Knox, Bryce, and Jusserand signed the treaties that called for "unlimited arbitration." At first Taft chose not to try to sell his idea—this radical departure in the conduct of American foreign policy—to the people directly. As he explained it, "I am not hunting this bird with a brass band . . . I do not want to stir up too much hostility toward it by being too eager for it."[25] Neither he nor Knox took any soundings of the attitude of the Senate. Somewhat surprisingly Knox, a former senator, did not approach members of the Committee on Foreign Relations of the upper house. Only in October did the president take his message of arbitration to the public disguising his swing across the country as a preelection move. It was to no avail.[26] The Senate fatally revised the two treaties with reservations. For example, it ruled out any arbitration regarding the admission of aliens into the United States and any interference with the practice and the power of the Monroe Doctrine. The vote to revise, and in effect to reject, the treaties was 76 to 3.[27] It was an inglorious defeat for the President and the treaties were dead on arrival at the White House. Taft refused to forward them to London or Paris. He had been taught a stern lesson, and at a considerable price, including diminished prospects of a return to office in 1912. The lesson was not that the Senate was right and he was wrong. Rather it was that the people had to be educated to understand that arbitration and not war must be the way to the future. And the more terrible the war, the greater likelihood that voters and the senators who spoke for them would come to accept the proposition that nations must learn to live together. This solution could not be achieved by moral suasion alone, but by a combination of high principles and the will to enforce them against wayward regimes.

NOTES

[1] Innes to Grey, quoted in Walter V. and Marie V. Scholes, *The Foreign Policies of the Taft Administration* (Columbia: University of Missouri Press, 1970), p. 14.

[2] Minger, *Taft, The Apprenticeship Years*, p. 178.

[3] Scholes, *The Foreign Policies*, p. 157.

[4] Taft to John Barrett, Dec. 4, 1908, Taft Papers, Library of Congress.

[5] Taft to Knox, Dec. 22, 1909, Pringle, *Taft*, II, 694.

[6] *Foreign Relations*, 1912, 1043-44.

[7] Dana G. Munro, *Intervention and Dollar Diplomacy in the Caribbean, 1900-1921* (Princeton: Princeton University Press, 1964), pp. 224-25.

[8] For a concise treatment, see Scholes, *Foreign Policies*, pp. 40-44.

[9] Taft to Helen Herron Taft, Oct. 10, 1909, Pringle, *Taft*, I, 462.

[10] Taft to Knox in Paolo Coletta, *The Presidency of William Howard Taft* (Lawrence, KS: University of Kansas Press, 1973), p. 176.

[11] Paolo Coletta, *The Presidency of William Howard Taft* (Lawrence, KS: University of Kansas Press, 1973), p. 176.

[12] Taft to A.P. Farquhar, Sept. 11, 1912, Pringle, *Taft*, II, 709.

[13] Taft to Prince Chun, July 19, 1909, *Foreign Relations*, 1909, p. 178.

[14] Pringle, *Taft*, II, 689.

[15] Coletta, *Taft*, p. 199.

[16] Burton, *William Howard Taft in the Public Service* (Melbourne, FL: Krieger Publishing Company, 1986), p. 93.

[17] Taft to Bradley, Feb. 27, 1911, in Coletta, *Taft*, p. 144.

[18] Donald F. Anderson, *William Howard Taft, A Conservative's Conception of the Presidency* (Ithaca: Cornell University Press, 1968), p. 143.

[19] Coletta, *Taft*, p. 147.

[20]   Herbert F. Wright, "Philander Knox," in Samuel E. Bemis, ed., *The American Secretaries of State and their Diplomacy* (New York: Pagent Books, 1958), IX, p. 346. Roosevelt agreed with Taft's position that Canada would become an adjunct. Taft to Roosevelt, Jan. 10, 1911. Pringle, *Taft*, p. 588. Roosevelt to Taft, Jan. 12, 1911, *Letters of Theodore Roosevelt*, Elting E. Morison, ed. (Cambridge, Harvard University Press, 1951-54), 8 volumes, vol. 7, p. 206.

[21]   Coletta, *Taft*, p. 168.

[22]   Taft at the Connecticut State Fair, Sept. 7, 1911, Anderson, *Taft*, p. 277.

[23]   Archibald Butt, *Roosevelt and Taft, The Intimate Papers of Archie Butt, Military Aide*, 2 vols. (New York: Doubleday, Doran, 1930), I, 365.

[24]   Ibid., II, 635

[25]   Ibid.

[26]   D. Anderson, *Taft*, p. 280; see also Scholes, *Foreign Policies*, n. 18, pp. 10-11.

[27]   Coletta, *Taft*, pp. 172-73.

4 . World Order In The Offing

Two distinct and provocative ironies overshadow William Howard Taft's response to the death of peace in 1914. Indeed, it is supremely ironic that only because of a war of such catastrophic proportions were statesmen, as well as the people, brought to a realization that the very foundation of world political order was threatened. And therefore a search for the means of preventing a renewed conflict between the powers must be found. Taft, the man of peace, more pronouncedly so than any of his contemporaries save Woodrow Wilson, and certainly the leading Republican peace advocate, was primed to take action. However, he lacked the necessary office and influence to help, in the company of other like-minded men, to bring order out of chaos. Ex-presidents, irrespective of their stature in public life, are hard-pressed to have a determining role in affairs of state. Taft's place in the peace effort of 1915-19 amply bears this out. It was not that he did not try, but that he was without official position that defeated him when it came to the adoption of a formula for maintaining peace in the postwar world. His failure while president to win aproval of his arbitration treaties increased the odds against gaining acceptance of a far more comprehensive plan for keeping the peace that he advanced in 1915.

The twentieth century opened on a somewhat optimistic note regarding the peaceful settlement of international disputes. This feeling was common among the leading European nations and, given European dominance in many parts of the world, the feeling was the more widespread. American official and public opinion was in phase with this belief that at last the great multinational wars could be assigned to history past. From 1815 on the major conflicts that had arisen were limited in scope, an encouraging sign. In the United States there had been present a long-standing sentiment that added up to peace at any price. This was the summary position of the American

Peace Society that had become an umbrella organization for various local peace advocacy groups in 1825. It was highly moralistic in its outlook and was deeply embarrassed, if not rendered totally ineffective, with the coming and fighting of the Civil War. The Society's leadership and membership were made up largely of genteel reformers, lacking in political know-how and influence. Only one Secretary of State, John Sherman, was associated with the Society. More to the point, William Howard Taft had taken no part in its activities and Woodrow Wilson became a member only in 1908.[1]

Reflecting the changed position of the United States in world affairs after 1898, there was a new found sense of striving after international accord, best represented by the Lake Mohonk conferences that at first, in 1895, were devoted to speaking platitudes on world peace. Within a decade, however, the conferences were increasingly concerned with peace efforts associated with international arbitration, a practical means formalized by treaty. This development made the prospect of world accord more appealing to practical-minded men, William Howard Taft among them. Arbitration provided a method for resolving disputes. This had long been an ad hoc procedure for the United States, dating back to 1871 and the Alabama claims. Now it was hoped that arbitration would take place under terms of dual or multilateral treaties. Method was to be wedded to morality with greater emphasis on the former consideration. Taft, who had always been a man of practical morality, was greatly attracted to arbitration as a concept, but as has been noted, it was but a step, admittedly a very important step, toward world diplomacy. His world order would rest, in Taft's vision, on a code of international law as adjudicated by a world court. What was entering into the mix of ideas, proposals, and expectations was old-fashioned diplomacy, to be equipped with new tools and a new outlook, viz., wars could be avoided by negotiation, studied compromise, and adjudication.[2]

As the peace movement went forward after 1905, men of the law, visionaries no doubt, became active supporters of world order, an understanding that led them to found the American Society of International Law. This Society was based on the conviction that world peace presupposed the reign of law. Such law must rest on a code, commonly agreed upon and enforced, with a court to pass judgment on cases brought before it. Arbitration required negotiation, whereas adjudication aspired to a higher level of justice. Taft followed such developments intently, judges in his mind being the men ideally trained to resolve disputes calmly and fairly.

Meanwhile the politics of the 1912 presidential election sent Taft from the White House to Yale, where he accepted the Kent Professorship of Law at his alma mater. Yale proved to be a place of public repose where the natural instinct of a scholarly mind asserted itself. Professor Taft wrote several books over the next three years, all of which dealt with public affairs. In the first of these, *Popular Government*, he addressed the problem of arbitration treaties, a problem because of the refusal of the Senate to pass into law the treaties he had presented to the upper house when he was president. Conscious of writing for an educated but popular audience he spoke his mind bluntly: "These treaties are practically nothing more than a general statement that we are in favor of arbitration of an issue when we agree to arbitrate it or, in other words, when we think it will be in our advantage to arbitrate it. Questions of national honor and of vital interest include all those questions, the agitation of which is likely to lead to war, and therefore, arbitration treaties which except such questions may be said to be treaties for the settlement of those questions that never would involve war in their settlement anyhow. This clearly shows that they are not adapted at all to the purpose of preventing war." In short, the amendments made to the treaties by the Senate rendered the treaties superfluous. Of course Taft had drafted the treaties in the first place to provide the means of avoiding wars among the United States, Britain and France.[3]

A second and more important book was *The President and His Powers.* Despite inferences that in some respects rebuked Theodore Roosevelt's conduct of the office, Taft's treatment on the whole was fair-minded. He has proven to be the only ex-president to write a scholarly analysis of the institution. One area of power that he discussed at length was treaty making. It may be said he was looking both to the past, the failed arbitration treaties with England and France, and to the immediate future, the struggle over ratification of the Treaty of Versailles, as prescient as that may seem.

The ex-president gave special attention to the power of the chief executive to shape and then conduct American foreign policy. During his tenure in office he pursued diplomatic initiatives in the Americas and in the Far East, sometimes in a highly personal way. His justification for so acting was that, unlike the congress that enjoyed only delegated powers, presidential power was not narrowly defined or restricted in matters of foreign policy. In this respect he insisted unequivocally that for a president "the first and most important duty he has is that of initiating and drafting treaties with foreign nations."[4] He cited particulars: the president has the sole authority in all foreign policy matters. And he and he alone can ratify and proclaim a treaty once the Senate has approved the terms of the document. He rejected the proposition that the Senate was more crucial to the treaty process than the chief executive.

Taft expanded his explanation of presidential authority in this matter by giving close attention to the afore discussed failed treaties with Britain and France. "The treaties provided," he contended, "that the countries concerned should submit all questions capable of judicial solution arising between them, which could not be settled by negotiation, to the decision of an arbitral tribunal under the treaty." Whereupon he took direct issue with the Senate on the grounds that the position it had assumed regarding the 1911 treaty proposals made it impossible to arbitrate a matter of difference between the United States and the two other nations involved. To reverse the course of Taft's argument: in giving approval to the proposed treaties which called for a preliminary tribunal regarding the question of arbitral action was no more than a case of construing the treaties. "It was only consenting to arbitrate construction of the treaties when the event occurs which requires construction." And he added, "this has been done numerous times already." Recall that Taft was writing with World War I well underway and men of peace were looking to the postwar world. Thus he wrote: "I think it is of the utmost importance that every one interested in the establishment of a League of Nations, for the settlement of differences between them by an international court should realize that the attitude of the Senate . . . would make it impossible for the United States to become a member of such a League." And he continued: "I am anxious therefore in season and out of season to argue as forcibly as I may the error of the Senate in this regard." Taft had thrown down the gauntlet. Only time would reveal whether the Senate would pick it up. But knowing as we do the ultimate outcome, Taft's warning had a prophetic ring.[5]

The ex-president closed his disection of the powers of the president in a singular way: "The Constitution does give the President wide discretion and great power and it ought to be so. . . . He is no figurehead and it is entirely proper that an energetic and active, clear-sighted people . . . should be willing to rely on their judgment in selecting him . . . and should entrust him with all power needed to carry out their governmental purpose, great though that may be." Taft was saying the president was a servant of the people—a notably Progressive pronouncement. Very likely this conviction had germinated years before, only to come to full flower when given the awesome responsibilities of being president with powers to act in behalf of his countrymen.[6]

The pious hopes for peace, the appeal of negotiated arbitration, and the vision of international lawyers melded, though not in equal portions, in the founding of the League to Enforce Peace. It was an audacious concept, in part because it broke ground in favor of world-ordered diplomacy and because it was originated and pushed forward by a band of private citizens rather than emanating from the White House or the Department of State. It had, in consequence, a grass roots quality, however distinguished were the men who were the prime movers in its establishment. If it appeared at first as one of several proposals to protect the nation-states from destruction by running on their own swords, the League became THE rallying point as its ranks swelled with peace advocates of various shades and differing nostrums. As the war went on, so did the League push hard for recognition as a fair but workable way to prevent the collapse of world order, an idea whose time had come. The driving force behind the League derived from the convictions of three men in particular. Henry Holt of *The Independent* was tireless in his organizational efforts. Theodore Marburg, who as early as 1910 had been instrumental in bringing into being The American Society for the Judicial Settlement of International Disputes, was an indispensable source of advice, which William Howard Taft had heartily endorsed. The third leader was William B. Howland of *Outlook*, a man wise in the ways of shaping public opinion. At a dinner meeting at the Century Club in New York City they discussed particulars of the formation of the League and came to a ready agreement on what had to be done and how to proceed. True, talk of such a body had begun immediately after the war had started in 1914 so that it can be said it was an evolutionary process that attained a decisive stage of growth by the January 25, 1915 dinner at the Century Club. But most of the early proposals called for a peace conference to end the war. Given the state of mind of all the combatants in 1914 and 1915, this was not going to happen, because they were too deeply enmeshed in a "victory over the

enemy" mentality. Out of the Century Club affair came the statement
that international disputes must not be settled with a resort to arms
"under the penalty of the employment against the offending nation of
the united forces of the League." It was to be sure embryonic, but it
possessed the vital signs of growth that produced a fully developed
draft proposal by the time the war was winding down.[7]

Prior to the Century Club meeting, Henry Holt and a number of
other peace advocates had produced a number of concrete suggestions
about how to meet the European crisis; in other words, ways of dealing
with the disaster were widespread. Theodore Marburg took the opportunity to inform both Taft and President Wilson of what he termed, at
that stage of developments, the League of Peace. What appealed to
Taft in particular was the statement: "The early creation of an
International Court of Justice is held to be especially important." But
could one be sure that such a court would have a meaningful existence
without an international police force, a standing army, so to speak? Taft
was taken aback by the second part of the proposal, only to be persuaded of its indispensability by A. Lawrence Lowell, the Harvard
University President and a stalwart defender of the League's enforcement role, by economic means and if need be by military action. The
ex-president was moving slowly but surely toward embracing in its
fullest meaning, world-ordered diplomacy.[8] Taft agreed to edit and
issue the resolutions of the conference, putting them in press release
form for the information of the public. The next step, agreed on at the
end of March, was an assembly of several hundred prominent citizens,
meeting at Independence Hall, Philadelphia on June 17, Bunker Hill
Day. Taft delivered a set of pregnant remarks on this occasion. He
advised his audience and the nation that the League did not seek to end
the war that was then raging, even though the *Lusitania* had been sunk
the month before with a considerable loss of American life. Admitting
that the complete abolition of war was impractical, nonetheless, he said:

"The threat of an overwhelming force by a great league with the will-ingness to make the threat good in order to frighten nations into the use of rational and peaceful means"[9] is a necessity. At the Philadelphia meeting Taft accepted the presidency of the League to Enforce Peace thereby committing himself to many months of struggle, not to make the world safe for democracy but rather to make it safe so that demo-cratic nations might live in peace. Taft was moving back into the political mainstream during one of the most agitated periods of his day, and doing so without an official position or the power to go with it, a sit-uation that could cost him dearly. But he was never to doubt his duty in this respect, his duty to mankind.

Over the next three years, by means of more than fifty speeches and newspaper articles, Taft sought to explain, promote, and justify the ideas of the League to Enforce Peace and to endorse President Wilson's league efforts. He came, thereby, to express a fully limned concept of world-ordered diplomacy. It must be understood that Taft's great cause was creation of a league along the lines of his league or that of Wilson once the president had spelled that out. Once the league concept was taken out of the realm of speculation and entered the real world of pol-itics and diplomacy, Taft was for a league. As closely as he was associated with the League to Enforce Peace he was fundamentally a league advocate, irrespective of its provenance. As long as it became a reality and the United States a full fledged member, Taft would have considered his work done, his mission fulfilled. To appreciate this posi-tion more fully it becomes necessary to examine the most instructive of his formal addresses and journalistic pieces. As he noted in his Foreward to the publication of spoken and written words as late as July, 1920, "I have nothing to recall in what is said in them."[10]

Even before the meeting at Independence Hall Taft had delivered an address at the World Court Congress in May of 1915. On this occa-sion he first argued from the history of the original American governmental organization. The colonies had evolved into states, and the states into a nation. This nationhood was singularly marked by the creation and power of a supreme court designed to settle disputes arising between the states and between the states and the national government. "The analogy between the function of the Supreme Court in hearing and deciding controversies between the states and that of an international tribunal sitting to decide a cause between sovereign nations is very close." To buttress his argument Taft spoke in great detail of the workability of the sovereign states in the American union living side by side, and he cited court decisions to undergird his position. Such a series of remarks might at first seem irrelevant in as much as no world court comparable in function to that of the United States Supreme Court was called for in the League. Nonetheless Taft was insistent that the lessons of history, viz., the evolution of the federal union into nationhood, in every respect not be lost on his audience.[11]

Although Taft spoke in general terms in his acceptance speech at Independence Hall, nonetheless he made several salient points that he believed his countrymen should be aware of. The first of these was that league members were bound to use the machinery of the league to settle a controversy likely to lead to war. Secondly, "we are not peace-at-any-price men" in proposing a league. Thirdly, issues that can be decided on principles of international law and equity are to be referred to a standing tribunal; nonjusticiable issues are to be referred to a Council of Conciliation. In light of these considerations Taft wisely observed: "We feel that we ought not to attempt too much," another intimation of the evolutionary character of his thinking about achieving world order.[12]

Taft was emboldened to take up the issue of constitutionality of the League at the May 1916, "First Annual Assemblage" of the League to Enforce Peace held in Washington. He drew on both presidential experience and his constitutional expertise as a onetime federal judge (and it may be added a future chief justice) to make his case. The familiar objection to a treaty that involved a judicial consideration he addressed at once. "Both upon reason and authority" the senatorial power to drastically revise a treaty was challenged. Taft chose to cite a case at law, *Geofrey vs. Riggs* 133U.S. 258, to this effect:

> That the treaty power of the United States extends to all proper subjects of negotiations between our Government and the Governments of other nations is clear. . . . The Treaty power . . . is in terms unlimited, except by those restraints which are found [in the Constitution]. . . . But with these exceptions, it is not perceived that there is any limit to the questions which can be adjusted touching any matter which is properly the subject of negotiation with a foreign country.

To which court judgment Taft added: "Issues that can be settled on principles of law and equity are proper subjects for decision by a judicial tribunal. Such issues have been settled by Boards of Arbitration, agreed to by independent sovereign states since there were governments." Jay's Treaty of 1795 he cited as the first of eighty-four international arbitrations to which the United States had been a party. In these cases it was never suggested the government was delegating any power at all to the tribunal. On the particular objection that a League alliance would take from Congress the power to declare war, Taft was at pains to point out that treaties between the United States and Panama and between the United States and Cuba contained the clause that "makes it the duty of the Government to declare war under certain conditions that may arise." Under Article II of the treaty with Cuba, the United States had the right to intervene, by military force if need be, to preserve Cuban independence. And this the United States did in 1906, with no outcry from the congress. What Taft was attempting to do was to overcome misunderstanding about the nature and

extent of the treaty authority.[13]   One bogeyman of the day was
Washington's maxim of "no entangling alliances." In an address before
the National Education Association in 1916, Taft asserted that "were
Washington living today he would not consider the League as an entangling alliance . . . while he did dwell, and properly dwelt, on the very
great advantage that the United States had in her isolation from
European disputes, it was an isolation which does not now exist."
America was now a world power, no longer isolated from Europe, and
could not be isolated because of America's world position.[14]

In the course of writing and delivering dozens of speeches, Taft
touched on very many aspects of the proposed peace process, such as
the place of international law in the scheme of things, disarmament on
land and on sea, the freedom of the seas for trading nations, the fate of
the colonial system, open diplomacy, Ireland and the League, to cite
but a few of the many he brought into public discourse. From this sam-
pling it is clear that some issues were more critical than others, yet all of
them were in keeping with the tenor of the times and addressed subjects deserving attention. But on two occasions in particular, in January
1917 and again in June 1918, he talked plainly and persuasively about
the purpose of the war, and thus of the League. In the first of these two
addresses Taft gave a sober, no frills statement about the aim and operation of the League, which deserves to be quoted fully:

> The purpose of the League to Enforce Peace is, after
> the present war, to organize the world politically so as to
> enable it to use its power to prevent the hotheadedness of
> any nation from lighting a fire of war which shall spread
> into another general conflagration. It proposes to effect
> this by securing membership in the League of all the great
> nations of the world. The minor stable nations will then
> certainly join because of the protection which the League
> would afford them against sudden attack by a great power.

The League will then become a World League. If it does
not, it will fail of its purpose. No member of the League is
to begin war against any other member until after the question between them shall have been submitted to a Court,
if the question is of a legal nature, or a Commission of
Conciliation, if it can not be settled on principles of law.
The members agree to await the judgment in the one case
or the recommendation of a compromise in the other,
before beginning hostilities. If any member violates this
agreement and begins hostilities before the appointed
time, the whole power of the League, by the joint use of
the military and naval force of its members, is to be exerted to defend the nation prematurely attacked against the
nation attacking it. The compulsion thus to be exercised is
directed only to securing deliberation and delay sufficient
to permit a hearing and judgment on questions of a legal
nature, and a hearing and recommendation of compromise
on other questions.[15]

From that beginning statement Taft went on to concede that there
would be practical difficulties in trying to enforce judgments and perhaps great difficulty in enforcing compromises. But at first, he said, the
League would be satisfied to secure agreement from the nations
involved, whereby hearings of potential causes of war would take place,
thus postponing and more likely preventing wars. In so saying Taft
reminded his listeners and readers alike—many of these talks were
printed in newspapers—that this would be a "long step forward" with
more steps to be taken as progress was made in this procedure.[16]

Taft believed it was essential for him to be plainspoken because he
found the very concept of a league was under fire from its opponents;
Theodore Roosevelt and Senator William Borah were singled out in this
respect. Either by design or by accident, these and other critics were

misrepresenting the purpose and usefulness of international cooperation. Both Roosevelt and Borah were ultranationalist in their outlook.

Some months later, in June 1918, he turned his attention once more
to basics. Again, to quote Taft, he said: "We are in the war, first of all,
to make the world a safer and a better place to live in. We are fighting
to bring about a lasting peace. There was a time when many cherished
the hope that such a peace could be established by the moral force of
public opinion. Now we know that peace has a more terrible price, and
we are ready to pay the price." The matter-of-fact tone of the 1917
address had altered in the face of the sacrifices involved in prosecuting
the military side of the conflict. Taft stressed that the war was not a
European war, but one involving the whole world: "We announced ourselves as citizens of the world when we declared war against Germany.
World politics, after all, are only fundamental questions of right and
wrong. We are fighting for the right against the wrong." Despite the
evenhanded character of many of Taft's remarks, he definitely came to
favor peace with victory. One address, given in Montreal in September
1917, he entitled "The Menace of a Premature Peace." He linked the
securing of permanent world peace with the defeat of German militarism and the destruction of the Hohenzollern dynasty. Peace could be
won only when the war was over and Germany defeated and not simply
by the cessation of the fighting. It was not a time for peacemaking, he
told his Canadian audience. The League was not a peacemaker and
should not intervene in the war. It would come into play when the war
was won and the disturbers of the peace put aside. Only then could the
world hope to embark on the path to peace. Taft it appears had caught
the wartime contagion and vented it, to the surprise of some, according
to newspaper reports. Nonetheless he continued his remarks by noting
that there was a liberal element in German people and culture. The
League would encourage the old enemy to value the era of peace that
would soon dawn. This was indeed a long speech and even as it is read

today it takes on some of the characteristics of a harangue against German militarism and German history in the late 19th century with its wars against Austria and France. In a final analysis this amounted to an indictment of the German nation issued by a judge familiar with that legal device.[17]

As 1916 gave way to 1917-18 and the United States was at war, Taft continued to put forward his ideas and opinions on any number of germane considerations regarding the issues raised by the war and the peace. On one occasion he spoke about "The Workingman and the War," and observed that it was the workers of the countries engaged in the conflict who had become "weary . . . [and] felt the suffering and dreadful pinch of starvation and want, their souls were gripped with a determination to have no more war." Or he spoke and wrote of religious liberty, laying particular stress on the plight of European Jewry: "On the whole, it is not too much to say that the people of the Jewish race [sic] have suffered more in this war, as noncombatants, than any other people, unless it be the Serbians and the Armenians."[18] This problem he brought up again, some months later. He had heard rumors emanating from Paris that a declaration in favor of religious tolerance had failed to win approval during a conference proceeding. Taft was quick to underscore the provision in the League Covenant "that in all countries which are to be governed by a mandatory of the League, the charter, under which the mandatory acts, shall require protection of religious freedom." Anti-semitism, at least as officially practiced, would be a thing of the past. Or Taft could be heard raising his voice for a free Ireland which a League, once in place and functioning, would attempt to bring about. At one juncture Taft spoke of dominion status for the whole of Ireland. In any case this was an example of Taft's recognition of and sympathy for the aspiring nationalities, who though small in numbers, deserved to be allowed to determine their own political future.[19]

Taft continued his speech-making once Wilson had gone to Paris to negotiate a treaty of peace, delivering some of his most resounding endorsements of a league and elucidating his vision of a postwar diplomatically ordered world.   In an article appearing in the Philadelphia *Public Ledger* for January 23, 1919, he asserted boldly: "The League of Nations Is Here," adding this crucial thought to his lead statement: it was up to the leaders and the people to make it a living thing.   In an article appearing a week later in the same newspaper, he wrote of the League "bite."   He quoted Lloyd George: "The best security for peace will be that nations will band themselves together to punish the peace-breaker."   And he added to that the stated position of Herbert Asquith, the former Liberal prime minister: the league must "make it their joint and several duty to repress by their united authority and, if need be, by their combined naval and military forces, any wanton aggressive invasion of the peace of the world."   In his expression of agreement with two leading British statesmen, Taft appeared to be thinking in terms of a league to enforce peace by the ultimate means available, viz., military action.   Mere resolutions of protest would be insufficient to meet the need in certain cases.   As he was at pains to say, "bite" was a Wilsonian expression.[20]

One of the most promising of the 14 Points dealt with the self-determination of peoples.   Taft addressed the problem directly and in doing so was being both idealistic and practical.   Issues such as the restriction of the Turkish domain, establishing Balkan boundary lines, securing freedom for Armenians—all these and others "will try the ingenuity of statesmen in working out a just result. . . . Who shall determine this?" he solemnly asked.   Having laid down a challenge he commented further:

> It becomes apparent at once that the general principle of popular rule is not a panacea and that many issues will have to be settled by the Congress of Nations [sic], according to

expedient and practical justice, over the objection of some
part of the people affected. The result will illustrate the
inherent error in the frequent assumption that a Government
by the people is a Government in which that which is done
is the will of each one. A practical Government by the people is a Government by a majority of the voters.

The unsparing language Taft used here was an indication of the difficulty of putting into effect the principle that people should have the
opportunity to exercise "self-determination"[21]

In the new peace setting there must be both disarmament by the
nations and freedom of the seas, topics brought up by Taft as part of his
overall approach to analyzing conditions in the postwar years. He wrote
that "Allied Powers must retain armament to constitute a police force to
secure peace between the new nations. . . . This will justify the United
States in maintaining a potential army by a system of universal training
. . . and increasing our navy." No starry-eyed idealist Taft, if he is frank
enough to speak out in this regard, so contrary was it to the American
tradition. Indeed in the whole range of his expressed opinions and proposals, this appears as both unexpected and highly controversial. But
honest as it well may have been, its effects would be more likely negative than positive. Or was Taft merely exercising his right to freedom of
expression as a private citizen and not as an officer of the government?[22]

At the same time the ex-president was appealing to the American
businessman, presumably largely Republicans, in a widely circulated
set of remarks given at the Commonwealth Club in San Francisco,
February 19, 1919. Details of the Covenant of the League of Nations
had been well publicized and discussed, which gave Taft the opportunity to urge its support by the business leaders in California and across
the nation. "I wish you would study that covenant. . . . It is a well conceived plan. It does not involve as much compulsory force as our
League to Enforce Peace has recommended, but it comes very near it;

and it carries with it an arrangement for amendment and for elasticity that, as experience goes on, will enable the League to adopt other methods." As for American participation in the League: "Our presence will give to the League a potential strength and prestige which it will not have without us. So it is our duty to join, if we want to see the thing through, if we want to be square with those who fought this war for three years for us."[23] Moving east across the nation Taft told an audience in St. Louis that the League of Nations was a barrier to any great war in the future. And because it will be compellingly impossible for the United States to remain uncommitted in any future European war, all the more reason why America should be an active, nay, a leading nation in the League.[24] Quite justifiably Taft understood the League as an evolving extension of the kind of great power arbitration he had proposed when president. Had further steps been taken in 1911-12 by the negotiation of arbitration treaties with Germany and Italy, which Taft had been willing to consider at that time, diplomacy might have triumphed in 1914. But under the alliance system as it was in place in 1914, peaceful resolution was impossible. Thoughts such as these were likely in his mind when he prepared to deliver a major foreign policy address upon an invitation from the President, at the Metropolitan Opera House in New York on March 4, 1919. At this time he offered a proposal, operable under the aegis of the League, in which nations would agree to a three-month cooling-off period after an arbitration ruling had been rendered, during which time a reasonable compromise might be reached. Again, it was one of those steps in the direction of the long sought peace on earth, spoken of from time immemorial, or at the very least, the high ground of an international political order based on noble principles and enforced by common agreement. Professor Woolsey had written to that effect in his book, *International Relations*, a study with which the young collegian had become very familiar. Both James Bryce and Lawrence Lowell, among his contemporaries, had concluded as much, thereby helping to confirm Taft's belief that this order and agreement was the best prospect for secure peace.[25]

William Howard Taft's statesmanship never showed to better advantage than it did in his address, "The Paris Covenant for a League of Nations," that March day. It was a mighty sound coming from deep within, equal to if not superior to any statement delivered by any Democrat or Republican who dealt with war and peace from 1914 to 1919. It must be read in its entirety if we are to come to a fuller awareness of how committed the speaker was to the Covenant as an integral part of the Versailles Treaty and how carefully crafted his arguments were in its behalf. It was that rarity of the political arena, a nonpartisan announcement that no other participant in the battle for the League articulated. Among the principal assertions made in promoting adherence of the United States to the Treaty and the League were the following: "Our Constitution contains no inhibition, express or implied, against" becoming part of the proposed world community of nations. Membership in the League will in no way nullify the effect of statutes passed in pursuance to the Constitution. The mechanism proposed for the peaceful settlement of contending claims takes into full account Congressional prerogatives. The Monroe Doctrine is neither supplanted nor weakened. Article X will not work to commit United States forces without Congressional approval. The sense of the nation is for peace and disarmament. The President of the United States has the authority under the Constitution to negotiate the timing and the content of treaties, and he alone enjoys that responsibility. Were the United States to forego membership in the League, the old alliance system and balance of power diplomacy would quickly reemerge. "We would witness a speedy recurrence of war in which the United States would be as certainly involved as it was in this war. . . . No critic of the League has offered a single constructive suggestion to meet the crisis that I have thus summarily touched upon." The Supreme Court, from

John Marshall onward, has held that the federal government is the sovereign government of the American people and is therefore the designate for carrying on diplomatic policy. Arbitration is an age-old device in our history of dealings with other nations. And finally a verbatim rendering of Taft's peroration:

> The League Covenant should be in the Treaty of Peace. It is indispensable if the war is to accomplish the declared purpose of this nation and of the world and if it is to bring the promised benefit to mankind. We know the President believes this and will insist upon including the Covenant. Our profound sympathy in his purpose and our prayers for his success should go with him in his great mission.[26]

President Wilson could not but have been moved by the invocation of prayerful support. Wilson's address that followed appealed to both emotion and common sense. It appeared that, for the moment, Democrats and Republicans might join hands and vote to approve the treaty and the League. Like all moments this moment passed, and within weeks it would be politics as usual, Democrats and Republicans at each other's throat.

At the time the League to Enforce Peace was organized, there were three prominent Republicans—granted of different outlooks on the war and the peace to follow—with whom Taft hoped to work to achieve the League's objectives: Elihu Root, Henry Cabot Lodge, and Theodore Roosevelt. He judged their support to be crucial, and of the three, Root was the most important to enlist. The Taft-Root friendship and their common political and legal values promised well for a meeting of minds. Sometime secretary of war and of state and New York senator, Root was widely respected for his grasp of international affairs as well as his belief that one day a code of international law, to be adjudicated by a world court, would be in place to deter, if not to obviate, the resort to war. And it is not too much to claim that Taft and Root enjoyed a mutual regard, and this despite Root's refusal to give full support to Taft's 1911 arbitration treaties. The exigencies of wartime, it was thought by the League's leadership, would surely find Root sympathetic to the enforcement of peace. Root was offered the vice presidency, under Taft, of The League to Enforce Peace, as well as board membership, but he refused both appointments. All of this did not augur well, particularly when the ex-president took up the cudgels for Wilson's version of an association of nations. Root made no secret of his objection to concerted military action on the part of the United States without the explicit approval of the congress. Reluctantly no doubt Taft had to accept Root as an internationalist in spirit but a nationalist in fact.

When President Wilson returned from Paris in February 1919 with a completed treaty, he proposed that Taft and Root join with him to explain and extoll the treaty at the March 4 nonpartisan gathering at the Metropolitan Opera house. Taft was only too glad to do so, such was his commitment to the idea of the League. He, in turn, wrote Root an invitation to join Wilson and him. In so doing he sought to re-enforce his position and to help the President strengthen the appeal to the American people of what was a major change in the nation's foreign policy. Thus he wrote Root:

> If you think you can support confirmation of the Paris
> convention, after amendments that will not destroy its sub-
> stance, I think it is your duty to join me in speaking with
> the President. . . . I have word from the White House that
> they are very anxious to secure your support.

To which invitation Root replied matter-of-factly: "Thanks. I think I will not attend."[27]

As the fight over the treaty got underway, Root never yielded on the issue of the use of American troops fighting in the name of a league, either Taft's or Wilson's version. And until mid-July 1919 Taft tried to keep the contest over the Versailles Treaty as nonpartisan as possible. In this endeavor he failed, of course. Only when he came to realize that politically there was no prospect of an unrevised treaty being approved by the Senate did he himself propose amendments, thus in a sense joining the reservationists, or so it appeared to Wilson.[28]

Oddly enough, in view of his overall efforts to gut the Versailles Treaty and the success he achieved in persuading the Senate to reject it in any form, Henry Cabot Lodge appeared to be a better bet, early on, to support the concept of a league of nations proposal. Like all public-minded men, Lodge was in search of a foreign policy for the United States that would do justice both to his own country and to the leading nations of the world. But as he once said: "When the relations of my country with other nations are involved I cannot yield to them. My politics has always stopped at the water's edge."[29] Yet as late as December 1916, Lodge appeared to be sitting on the fence when it came to American participation in some kind of association of nations. He delivered an address worthy of note in this regard in June 1916 at Union College. Excerpts from his remarks bear this out:

> What can we do in the larger sense toward securing and maintaining the peace of the world?" he asked the Union College graduates. "This is a . . . difficult question, but turn it back and forth as we may there is no escape from the proposition that the peace of the world can only be maintained as the peace and order of . . . the world. Nations must unite as men unite to preserve peace and order. The great nations must be so united as to be able to say to any single country, 'You must not go to war'; and they can only say that effectively when the country desiring war knows that the force which the united nations place behind peace is irresistible. . . .

It may seem utopian at this moment to suggest a union
of civilized nations in order to put a controlling force behind
the maintenance of peace and international order; but it is
through the aspiration for perfection, through the search for
utopias, that the real advances have been made. At all
events, it is along this path that we must travel if we are to
attain in any measure to the end we all desire of peace on
earth [sic]. It is at least a great, a humane purpose to which,
in these days of death and suffering, of misery and sorrow
among so large a portion of mankind, we might well dedi-
cate ourselves. We must begin our work with the clear
understanding that our efforts will fail if they are tainted
with the thought of personal or political profit or with any
idea of self-glorification; we may not now succeed, but I
believe that in the slow process of the years others who come
after us will reach the goal. The effort and the sacrifice
which we make will not be in vain when the end in sight is
noble, when we are striving to help mankind and lift the
heaviest burdens from suffering humanity.[30]

And there is more. At the first annual assembly of The League to
Enforce Peace, which met in Washington that year, Lodge joined Wilson
in probing the issues of world peace and the methods to be pursued to
achieve that end as the following words indicate clearly enough:

The limit of voluntary arbitration has, I think, been
reached. . . . I think the next step is that which this League
proposes and that is to put force behind international peace,
an international league or agreement, or tribunal, for peace.
We may not solve it in that way, but if we cannot solve it in
that way it can be solved in no other. . . .

The way in which this problem must be worked out . . .
must be left to this League and to those who are giving

this great question the study which it deserves. . . . I know how quickly we shall be met with the statement that this is a dangerous question . . . that no nation can submit to the judgement of other nations. . . . I know the difficulties that arise when we speak of anything which seems to involve an alliance.

But I do not believe that when Washington warned us against entangling alliances he meant for one moment that we should not join with the other civilized nations of the world if a method could be found to diminish war and encourage peace.

If our aspirations are for that which is great and beautiful and good and beneficent to humanity, even when we do not achieve our end, even if the results are little, we can at least remember Arnold's lines:

"Charge once more, then, and be dumb!
Let the victors, when they come,
When the forts of folly fall,
Find your body by the wall."[31]

It is unfair to dismiss these two public statements as "mere talk." It is true, however, that even as he spoke he was taking political aim at the President, his purpose being to defeat Wilson's 1916 re-election bid. And it is necessary to add that he wrote privately that he was "fighting shy" of the league idea. That was in October. By the end of the year he expressed a positive attitude toward a league but not anything that Woodrow Wilson would conjure up. In a letter to James Bryce, one of the most respected British advocates for a postwar association of nations, Lodge wrote: "What can be done with a league of peace in the future I do not know. We must try our best but the obstacles are enormous."[32] Yet the closer President Wilson got to reshaping his original league proposals in keeping with the suggestions of Taft and Lowell, the more Lodge was led to denounce the amended document. That it was insufficiently Americanized is only a partial explanation of Lodge's position. When personal dislikes are mixed with envy and then leavened with bitterness of partisan politics, the result is an unyielding obduration, delineated by the "water's edge."

The most distinguished of the leading Republicans whose opposition to the league Taft had to contend with was Theodore Roosevelt, yet he proved to be the least formidable. In some ways it is surprising that TR was dismissive of arbitration in light of the great success his arbitration proposal to Great Britain had achieved in the settlement of the Alaska boundary dispute in 1903. It may be argued that since he had been able to rig the commission by appointing the three Americans, none of whom was a jurist of note, as had been agreed by London, that this may have convinced him of the fatal flaw of the arbitration process. But the league idea was distinctive it itself. When he accepted the Nobel Prize in 1910, Roosevelt was heard to speak out in favor of such an institution. "It would be a master stroke if these great powers honestly bent on peace would form a League of Peace, not only to keep the peace among themselves but to prevent, by force if necessary, its being broken by others."[33] With the onset of the Great War Roosevelt had altered his outlook drastically. There is a combination of reasons for this. TR was the most intemperate and outspoken critic of President Wilson's diplomacy of neutrality, his frenzy partly inspired by his lack of official position and authority. He had fallen under the spell of wartime romanticism, convinced that he wanted to "raise a regiment" and set off for the Western Front, once the United States had entered the war. Wilson's neutrality stance consistently frustrated his dream of being in action once again. Finally Roosevelt was to die in January 1919, before the battle over the Treaty with the League had entered its crucial stage, but not before he had cast himself in the unaccustomed and unworthy role of a spoiler. His *bête noire* was Woodrow Wilson, and as with the more rabid Republicans, he thought in terms of Wilson-Taft proposals regarding war and peace.[34]

More to the point, Theodore Roosevelt was so complete a nationalist that any league sounded a false note. He took sharp issue with the League to Enforce Peace in a December 2, 1917 issue of the *Kansas City Star.* He wrote that it was mere hypocrisy to talk about enforcing the future peace when Taft saw the league not as use of force to stop or end war, but only as a means of preventing future wars.[35] Accordingly Roosevelt dismissed Wilson's dictum of "peace without victory" which was saying to the Germans, referred to in the *Star* article as murderers, that they were not being penalized or punished for starting the war in the first place.[36] In a letter to H. Rider Haggard written in early December, 1918, Roosevelt put it all very succinctly: "I am not at all sure about the future . . . I don't put much faith in the League of Nations or any corresponding cure-all."[37]

For the good of the nation and in defense of his fundamental belief in the attainability of a world-ordered diplomacy, Taft chose not to challenge in public forums the likes of minor anti-Wilsonites. He was not only willing but eager to argue against what they stood for by disputing the Round Robin idea of Henry Cabot Lodge, as it had been clothed in carefully worded language by Philander Knox, Taft's secretary of state who had become a senator from Pennsylvania in 1914. Lodge had introduced the Round Robin, reservations to the treaty written large, on March 4, 1919, just as the congress was to adjourn. Within a week, speaking to the Economics Club in New York City, Taft struck back at the attempt to separate the peace treaty and the league covenant in an address he termed "An Answer to Senator Knox's Indictment." Taft's address was much like a lawyer's brief although there were passages of excoriation as, for example, "the whole structure of Senator Knox's indictment falls." Or "I submit in all fairness that there never was a more palpable *nonsequitur* than this." What in particular was singled out for his scornful attention? The power of the executive council of the league (it had not executive power), the League's war-making power (it could only recommend, and a recommendation is not a declaration), nations were bound to act in military concert (each nation interpreted the meaning of the covenant), there is no supreme court (because the covenant is not a constitution), the war making power for the United States is not located in Geneva but in Washington. Taft's words and his spirit were a sure sign of the validity of the covenant and of his sustained effort to make the nation and the Senate come to realize the role of the United States in a freely ordered world.[38]

The very next month, writing in the *Public Ledger* for April 12, Taft again addressed the issues raised by the Round Robin, this time in more measured terms but with the same purpose in mind, that is, to show that the objections the Senate had raised to certain parts of the treaty and the covenant were no longer pertinent in view of the changes Wilson had managed to have interpolated into the text of the document. Allow Taft's dispassionate logic to disarm the signatories of the Round Robin to speak:

> If the cabled information as to the character of the amendments adopted is reliable, we may now confidently hope that the Senators who signed the Round Robin will be able to vote for the League as it is amended without being embarrassed in any degree by their signatures to that document. It will be remembered that they merely said that the Covenant in its then form was unacceptable to them, which of course does not prevent their consistently supporting the Covenant as at present amended. The further statement in the Round Robin was that they thought the peace treaty ought to be adopted at once and that the League should be postponed for further consideration. Of course such a view, which rested on the importance of hav-

ing peace come at once without delaying it for the sake of framing a league of nations covenant, ceases to apply when the peace treaty has been signed, with the League of Nations Covenant as a part of it, and indeed as an indispensable condition to its effective enforcement. The Round Robin Senators may well say that the second objection is removed, because now to insist upon opposing or amending the League, which is web and woof of the peace treaty submitted to them, is to postpone peace rather than to expedite it.[39]

Unfortunately over the coming months emotion would overcome logic as the determining element in the struggle for a league of nations, of whatever description. Taft strove to keep discussion and disagreement on a high plane. In the effort he was frustrated by both the Round Robin mentality of the Lodge-led Senate and the implacable determination of President Wilson to preserve the treaty exactly as it was when he presented it to the Senate in May 1919. Taft was caught between these two opposing forces. Convinced after weeks of wearing contention of the wisdom of compromise, but before Wilson had his physical collapse, he agreed to accept some reservations in the sincere belief that there was to be no other road the United States could travel in the quest for a world ordered by diplomacy. But the ultimate decision was not in his hands. The evolution of ideal diplomacy had fully matured in his mind only to remain unfulfilled in time and space. A decade after his death America was at war again, fighting to make real what William Howard Taft had never ceased believing in, a world-ordering diplomacy.

NOTES

1   Merle Curti, *Peace or War: the American Struggle, 1636-1936* (New York: W.W. Norton, 1936) has important chapters dealing with the struggle over the League of Nations. Edson L. Whitney, *The American Peace Society, a Centennial History* (Washington: The American Peace Society, 1936) is a detailed study, sympathetically presented, and a useful reference source.

2   C. Roland Marchand, *The American Peace Movement and Social Reform, 1898-1918* (Princeton, NJ: Princeton University Press, 1972) is a full-dress history covering the years 1898-1918, demonstrating the professionalization of the peace movement. Ruhl J. Bartlett, *The League to Enforce Peace*, (Chapel Hill: University of North Carolina Press, 1944) is a sharply focused and altogether comprehensive study of the promise and disappointment of a remarkable effort to win the peace.

3   William Howard Taft, *Popular Government, Works*, vol. V, p. 157.

4   William Howard Taft, *The President and His Powers, Works*, vol. VI, p. 81.

5   Ibid., p. 83

6   Frederick C. Hicks, *William Howard Taft, Yale Professor of Law and New Haven Citizen* (New Haven: Yale University Press, 1945) affords background and context for appreciating these years of scholarly activity.

7   Pringle, *Taft*, II, 929-39 gives an in-depth account of Taft's leadership role in founding and directing the work of the League.

8   Bartlett, *The League to Enforce Peace*, p. 36.

9   Ibid., pp. 44-49.

10   William Howard Taft, *Taft Papers on League of Nations*, in *Collected Works*, VII, xiii.

11   Ibid., "Plan for a League of Nations to Enforce Peace," pp. 38-39.

12   Ibid., "Proposals of the League to Enforce Peace," pp. 51-53.

13   Ibid., "Constitutionality of the Proposals," pp. 55-61.

14   Ibid., "A Constructive Plan for Human Betterment," pp. 68-69.

15   Ibid., "The Purposes of the League," pp. 73-74.

16   Ibid., p. 74.

17   Ibid., "Our Purpose," pp. 120-22.

18   Ibid., "Workingmen and the League," p. 138; "The League of Nations and Religious Liberty," p. 154.

19   Ibid., "Religious and Racial Freedom," p. 283; "Ireland and the League," pp. 210-12.

20   Ibid., "The League of Nations Is Here," p. 197; "The League's 'Bite,'" pp. 201-02.

21   Ibid., "Self Determination," pp. 123-24.

22   Ibid., "Disarmament of Nations and Freedom of the Seas," pp. 150-51.

23   Ibid., "To Business Men," p. 225; "From an Address at Salt Lake City, February 22. 1919," p. 232.

24   Ibid., "League of Nations as Barrier to Any Great Wars in Future," p. 237.

25   Ibid., "The Paris Covenant for a League of Nations 2," pp. 241-54.

26   Ibid., pp. 242, 249, and 254. For a succinct statement of Knox's position on the League see Herbert F. Wright, "Philander C. Knox," in *American Secretaries of State and Their Diplomacy*, IX, 350-57.

27   Richard W. Leopold, *Elihu Root and the Conservative Tradition* (Boston, Little Brown and Company, 1954), pp. 134-35.

28   For further consideration of the Taft-Wilson "partnership," see Burton, *Taft, Wilson and World Order*, p. 119.

29   Karl Schriftgiesser, *The Gentleman from Massachusetts: Henry Cabot Lodge* (Boston: Little Brown and Company, 1944), p. 269.

30   Ibid., pp. 271-73.

31   Ibid., pp. 276-77.

32   William C. Widenor, *Henry Cabot Lodge and the Search for an American*

Foreign Policy (Berkeley: University of California Press, 1980), p. 227.

33   Theodore Roosevelt, *Works* (New York: Scribner's, 1924), vol. 18, p. 414.

34   Philip C. Jessup, *Elihu Root*, 2 vols. (New York: Dodd, Mead & Company, 1938) II, 398.

35   *Roosevelt in the Kansas City Star; War-time Editorials by Theodore Roosevelt.* Ralph Stout, Editor (Boston: Houghton Mifflin Co., 1921), December 3, 1917, p. 61.

36   Ibid., October 30, 1918, p. 248.

37   Roosevelt to H. Rider Haggard, December 6, 1918, *Works of Theodore Roosevelt*, vol. 24, p. 547.

38   Taft, "Answer to Senator Knox's Indictment," Taft *Works*, VII, 255-62.

39   Ibid., "The Round Robin," pp. 279-80.

5 . CONSERVATIVE INTERNATIONALIST

Taft's appointment as chief justice brought a virtual end to his life in diplomacy and the politics that had been part of it. In the course of his fight for the League—or it might better be said, a league—he had shown himself consistent in the belief that the day had arrived not simply for peace efforts but for a mechanism to preserve world order. Taft had bred into him a respect for law, constitutional and statute, which would bring about a disciplined international community, just as it had for a domestic society in the advanced nations. He would have been the first to admit that it would be a quantum leap to have achieved world order by means of a league as proposed in 1919. In keeping with the lesson he drew from his personal experience in diplomacy, that is, the evolution of the idea of balance of power to international law, Taft had intimated and on occasion stated plainly that it was a stage by stage process. As the League grew in respect and in strength, based on initial success, it would mature to the point that peace among the great nations and their political or economic dependencies would come about. Taft's public philosophy was one of *con-serving*, a concept devoid of political overtones. Yet he took the real world for what it was at the time. The old order appeared to be broken as revolution swept Russia and threatened to inundate eastern Europe, and possibly Germany. The Old World, along with the New, must rethink the meaning of their histories in order to deal with the memories of the Great War and the questions left by its outcome. Thus Taft held out some hope that with a Republican president in office the issue of the league would be reconsidered and acted upon positively, such was his belief in the imperative of organized international cooperation. Instead, and this may well have been President Harding's most influential long-term decision, he nominated William Howard Taft to be Chief Justice of the Supreme Court. And Taft proceeded to reform the court system, reordering its priorities and its procedures, rendering it more responsive to the needs of a changing nation, and succeeding in all this to a remarkable degree.

No sooner was Taft in office than he was asked to help in the arbitration of a boundary between Panama and Costa Rica. Hostilities had broken out between these neighbors, tensions having been building for some years. Acting under treaty obligations between the two countries, Chief Justice White, Taft's predecessor, had ruled that Panama had to surrender the territory in question to Costa Rica; however, he neglected to name two surveyors who were to draw the boundary line as required by the arbitration ruling. After consultation with Secretary of State Hughes, Taft completed the work of the arbitration process. A small responsibility for the new chief justice, but one that no doubt gave him satisfaction.[1]

In the summer of 1922, Taft and his wife took an informal trip to England and it proved to be something akin to a state visit. They were received by King George and Queen Mary and later dined with their majesties at the American embassy. At the table, the King brought up the subject of the war debt and opined that if not forgiven it should at least be scaled down. Taft fended off this royal suggestion, saying that either such move would be very unpopular with the American public. The subject was again broached by Lloyd George at a luncheon at 10 Downing Street, the Welsh Wizard playing all his cards. He faulted Wilson's decision to go to Paris in person to negotiate a peace treaty, stressing that the president was not prepared for tough bargaining. When the debt issue surfaced the prime minister warned that the debt burden would lead to the collapse of a number of European nations, Germany in particular, which would be an invitation to Bolshevism. He appealed to Taft to pressure Secretary of State Hughes to have the United States send a representative to a conference soon to be called to consider the German debt problem. But his plea was to no avail. Taft as chief justice felt it inappropriate for him to become involved, whatever his personal feelings. As he later reflected on the visit, he felt he had promoted to some degree good feelings between England and America, one of his objectives when proposing the Anglo-American arbitration treaty in 1911.[2]

Taft did maintain an active interest in the Permanent Court of International Justice and possible United States participation in its deliberations. But, as had happened with the League, partisan politics again intruded. Secretary Hughes had asked Taft to determine if the United States could be party to the Court without assuming the obligations of League membership. A good deal of private diplomacy ensued: exchanges of ideas between Hughes and Taft, between Taft and Root, between Root and Sir Robert Cecil, the latter keenly supportive of American membership. Taft both as chief justice and as a peace advocate was strongly attracted, but not optimistic that Court membership would come about. The Senate approved membership so long as any American case going to the Court had a two-thirds approval by the upper house. It became a study in appearances and reality, and Taft gave up on it. Perhaps partly to save face he noted: "This question of the World Court and the League of Nations has become so distinctively political that being on the Bench I must avoid activity in it."[3]

Such activities were, of course, peripheral to Taft's duties as chief justice. But each of these involvements speaks to his concern for world peace, if not as an outcome of a grand design, then by such personal methods as arbitration and individual diplomatic actions. In fact, he might have surveyed the 1920s as the decade came to a close to find encouraging signs: the Washington Naval Conference, the spirit of Locarno, the Kellogg-Briand Peace Pact. Alas, there were counter indicators as well. The economic disruptions caused by the war remained unadjusted, the old alliance mentality continued to assert itself under the mantle of the League of Nations, and Woodrow Wilson's appeal for international cooperation was mocked by the isolationist stance of the United States. And finally, the year before Taft's death, the Japanese invaded Manchuria. This constituted a cardinal breach of the League Covenant. As Taft had so sagely predicted, were there to be another great war between Powers, the United States, perforce, would be drawn into that struggle. Such was his vision in matters of foreign affairs, a vision that brimmed with promise from 1915 to 1919 as he pursued the chimera of world-ordered diplomacy.

There were three separate but successive steps in the making of, and therefore in an understanding of William Howard Taft's conduct of, diplomacy. His family breeding and his schooling at Yale and in the law in Cincinnati account for his determination to support the rule of law, ever and always. Years in the Philippines and at the War Department fed his self-confidence in carrying out public policy in both diplomatic and domestic affairs. As president, Taft pursued what he considered to be a conservative middle course in both major foreign policy initiatives, Canadian reciprocity and Anglo-French arbitration treaties. Defeat of both proposals did not dissuade him from the belief that his position was justified. Elements both psychological and factual derived from defeat—as he estimated them—were discernible in his endorsement and leadership of The League to Enforce Peace. His platform of idealism and practicality shows Taft to have been a statesman ahead of his time once efforts got underway to reshape the contours of the international community after World War II. This was not so much in the details of a new organization as it was in the vision he had of a latter-day league of nations.

NOTES

[1]   Charles Evans Hughes to Taft, 25, 1921, quoted in Alpheus Thomas Mason, *William Howard Taft, Chief Justice* (New York: Simon and Schuster, 1964), p. 272.

[2]   Pringle, *Taft,* II, 1000-06.

[3]   Mason, *Taft, Chief Justice*, pp. 285-86.

BIBLIOGRAPHY

Alonso, Oscar. *Theodore Roosevelt and the Philippines 1897-1909*. Quezon City: University of Philippines Press, 1970.

"Alphonso Taft," in *Dictionary of American Biography*. Dumas Malone, ed. New York: Charles Scribner's Sons, 1936. Vol. 18, pp. 264-65.

Anderson, Donald F. *William Howard Taft: A Conservative's Conception of the Presidency*. Ithaca: Cornell University Press, 1960.

Anderson, Judith I. *William Howard Taft, an Intimate History*. New York: W.W. Norton, 1981.

Bartlett, Ruhl J. *The League to Enforce Peace*. Chapel Hill: University of North Carolina Press, 1944.

Burton, David H. *The Learned Presidency*. Madison, NJ: Fairleigh Dickinson University Press, 1988.

Taft, Wilson and World Order. Madison, NJ: Fairleigh Dickinson University Press, 2003.

Theodore Roosevelt: Confident Imperialist. Philadelphia: University of Pennsylvania Press, 1968.

William Howard Taft in the Public Service. Melbourne, FL: Krieger Publishing Company, 1986.

Butt, Archibald. *Roosevelt and Taft, The Intimate Papers of Archie Butt*, 2 vols. New York: Doubleday, 1930.

Campbell, Charles S. "The Bering Sea Settlement of 1892," *Pacific Historical Review* XXXII (Nov. 1963), 34-67.

Coletta, Paolo. *The Presidency of William Howard Taft*. Lawrence, KS: University of Kansas Press, 1973.

Cotton, Edward H. *William Howard Taft: A Character Study*. Boston: Beacon Press, 1932.

Curti, Merle. *Peace or War: The American Struggle 1636-1936*. New York: W.W. Norton, 1936.

DeSantis, Vincent. *The Shaping of Modern America 1877-1920*. St. Louis: Forum Press, 1977.

Duffy, Herbert. *William Howard Taft*. New York: Minton, Balch & Co., 1930.

Farrell, John T. "Background of the Taft Mission." *Catholic Historical Review*, April 1957.

The Federal Reporter. St. Paul: West Publishing Co., 1880-1924.

Foreign Relations of the United States. Washington, DC: United States Government Printing Office, 1912.

Gabriel, Ralph H. *The Course of American Thought*. New York: Ronald Company, 1940.

Gates, John Morgan. *Schoolbooks and Krags: The United States Army in the Philippines, 1898-1902*. Westport, CT: Greenwood Press, 1973.

Goebel, D. B. *American Foreign Policy*. New York: Holt, Rinehart, and Winston, 1961.

Griswold, A. Whitney. *The Far Eastern Policy of the United States*. New Haven: Yale University Press, 1938.

Guggenheim, Harry F. *The United States and Cuba: A Study in International Relations*. New York: Macmillan, 1934.

Healy, David. *United States Expansion: The Imperialist Urge, The 1890s*. Madison: University of Wisconsin Press, 1970.

Hicks, Frederick C. *William Howard Taft Yale Professor and New Haven Citizen*. New Haven: Yale University Press, 1945.

Hofstadter, Richard. *Social Darwinism in American Thought*. Boston: Beacon Press, 1969.

Keller, Albert G. *Reminiscences of William Graham Sumner*. New Haven: Yale University Press, 1927.

Jessup, Philip C. *Elihu Root*, 2 vols. New York: Dodd Mead & Co., 1938.

Leopold, Richard W. *Elihu Root and the Conservative Tradition*. Boston: Little Brown and Company, 1956.

Lockmiller, David. *Magoon in Cuba.* Chapel Hill: University of North Carolina Press, 1938.

Malloy, W.W. *Treaties, Conventions, International Acts, Protocols, Agreements.* Washington: Government Printing Office, 1923.

Manners, William. *TR and Will.* New York: Harcourt Brace, 1969.

Marchand, C. Roland. *The American Peace Movement and Social Reform.* Princeton: Princeton University Press, 1972.

Mason, Alpheus Thomas. *William Howard Taft, Chief Justice.* New York: Simon and Schuster, 1964.

May, Ernest. *Imperial Democracy.* New York: Harcourt Brace World, 1961.

McMath, Robert C. *American Populism.* New York: Hill & Wang, 1993.

Miller, Stuart C. *Benevolent Assimilation.* New Haven: Yale University Press, 1984.

Minger, Ralph. *William Howard Taft and American Foreign Policy: The Apprentice Years, 1900-1908.* Urbana: University of Illinois Press, 1975.

Munro, Dana G. *Intervention and Dollar Diplomacy in the Caribbean, 1900-1921.* Princeton: Princeton University Press, 1964.

Painter, Nell. *Standing at Armageddon: United States, 1877-1919.* New York: W.W. Norton, 1989.

Pringle, Henry F. *The Life and Times of William Howard Taft,* 2 vols. New York: Farrar and Rinehart, 1939.

Roosevelt, Theodore. *Letters of Theodore Roosevelt,* 8 vols., Elting E. Morison, ed. Cambridge: Harvard University Press, 1951-1954.

Roosevelt, Theodore. *Works,* 24 vols. New York: Charles Scribner's Sons, 1924.

Russell, Charles, and E.B. Rodriguez. *The Hero of the Philippines.* New York and London: Century Company, 1923.

Scholes, Walter V., and Maria V. Scholes. *The Foreign Policies of the Taft Administration.* Columbia: University of Missouri Press, 1970.

Schriftgiesser, Karl. *The Gentleman from Massachusetts: Henry Cabot Lodge*. Boston: Little Brown and Company, 1944.

Starr, Harris E. *William Graham Sumner*. New York: Henry Holt, 1925.

Stout, Ralph, ed. *Roosevelt in the Kansas City Star; Wartime Editorials by Theodore Roosevelt*. Boston: Houghton Mifflin Co., 1921

Sumner, William Graham. *Earth, Hunger and Other Essays*. New Haven: Yale University Press, 1939.

Taft, William Howard, *The Collected Works*, 8 vols., David H. Burton, ed. Athens, Ohio: Ohio University Press, 2001-2004.

   Popular Government. New Haven: Yale University Press, 1913.

   The President and His Powers. New York: Columbia University Press, 1924.

Whitney, Edson. *The American Peace Society*. Washington: The American Peace Society, 1936.

Widenor, William C. *Henry Cabot Lodge and the Search for an American Foreign Policy*. Berkeley: University of California Press, 1980.

Wiebe, Robert H. *The Search for Order*. New York: Hill & Wang, 1984.

Wiener, Philip. *Evolution and the Founders of Pragmatism*. Cambridge: Harvard University Press, 1949.

Wolff, Lon. *Little Brown Brothers*. Garden City: Doubleday, 1961.

Woolsey, Theodore D., *Introduction to the Study of International Law*. New York: Charles Scribner's Sons, 1883.

Wright, Robert F. "Philander Knox." *American Secretaries of State and Their Diplomacy*. Samuel E. Bemis, gen. ed. New York: Pageant Books, 1958.

Unpublished Sources

Taft Papers, Manuscript Division, Library of Congress.

Yale College Records, Yale Archives.

APPENDICES

THE TAFT-KATSURA AGREEMENT (1905)

Bringing about an understanding between the United States and Japan concerning large issues regarding balance of power in the Far East amounted to nothing less than a breakthrough for American presence in Asia. Its importance was enhanced by reason of the inclusion of Great Britain in what amounted to power-sharing in that part of the world.

. . . COUNT KATSURA and Secretary Taft had a long and confidential conversation on the morning of July 27 . . . .

First, in speaking of some pro-Russians in America who would have the public believe that the victory of Japan would be a certain prelude to her aggression in the direction of the Philippine Islands, Secretary Taft observed that Japan's only interest in the Philippines would be, in his opinion, to have these islands governed by a strong and friendly nation like the United States. . . . Count Katsura confirmed in the strongest terms the correctness of his views on the point and positively stated that Japan does not harbor any aggressive designs whatever on the Philippines . . . .

Second, Count Katsura observed that the maintenance of general peace in the extreme East forms the fundamental principle of Japan's international policy. Such being the case, . . . the best, and in fact the only, means for accomplishing the above object would be to form good understanding between the three governments of Japan, the United States, and Great Britain. . . .

Third, in regard to the Korean question Count Katsura observed that Korea being the direct cause of our war with Russia, it is a matter of absolute importance to Japan that a complete solution of the peninsula question should be made as the logical consequence of the war. If left to herself after the war, Korea will certainly draw back to her habit of improvidently entering into any agreements or treaties with other powers, thus resuscitating the same international complications as existed before the war. In view of the foregoing circumstances, Japan feels absolutely constrained to take some definite step with a view to precluding the possibility of Korea falling back into her former condition and of placing us again under the necessity of entering upon another foreign war. Secretary Taft fully admitted the justness of the Count's observations and remarked to the effect that, in his personal opinion, the establishment by Japanese troops of a suzerainty over Korea to the extent of requiring that Korea enter into no foreign treaties without the consent of Japan was the logical result of the present war and would directly contribute to permanent peace in the East. His judgment was that President Roosevelt would concur in his views in this regard, although he had no authority to give assurance of this.

————

This document, dated July 29, 1905, was "an agreed memorandum" of a conversation between Count Katsura, Prime Minister of Japan, and William Howard Taft, personal representative in Japan of President Theodore Roosevelt, who later gave his full approval of the agreement. Miscellaneous Letters of the Department of State, July, Part III, 1905.

THE HAVANA SPEECH (1906)

In his address at the University of Havana, attended by a large audience of influential Cubans and by students and professors, Taft was really seeking to export the principle that successful representative governments rest on the possession of private property by a working majority of the population of any given country. He urged the future generation of Cuban youth to embrace and live by the capitalist system which would produce and protect liberty.

Ladies and Gentlemen and Members of the University of Havana: I account it a particular honor in a moment of temporary place, representing the Executive of this Island, to take part in the exercises of this great University. It is of special interest and honor to me because it was my very good fortune when exercising the Executive function in the Philippine Islands in the Antipodes to take part in a similar function in a University founded by the same Order, and under similar influences, more than 100 years before this University was founded. I refer to the University of St. Thomas of Manila, founded by the order of the Dominicans, and still continued under that authority.

Members of the Latin race are accustomed and not without reason, to characterize those of the Anglo-Saxon race, as abrupt and conceited in our view of our power of pushing civilization. But those of us who have occasion to come close to the civilization of the Spanish race and its descendents, have had born in upon us the consciousness that the Anglo-Saxon race has much to learn from the intellectual refinement, the logical faculties, from the artistic temperament, from the poetic imagery, from the high ideals, and from the courtesy of the Latin and Spanish races.

One must know the history of these colonies to realize the tremendous force that Spain has exerted in the civilization and progress of the world. But nations, like men, suffer action and reaction. The great public works that Spain has erected the world over, testify to her patience and enterprise in centuries when we of the Anglo-Saxon world were struggling with something much less pretentious. The history of the early Spanish navigators and of her early colonies grows on one as it is studied. But the civilization of Spain, her civil life and all her institutions were founded on the idea of the control of one man or a few men in the state, and that idea has ceased to have force in the world. In the Anglo-Saxon world the principle was early brought to the front that those of the people who had education enough to know what their interests were, were more safely to be trusted with determining how those interests should be preserved than one man or a few men, however altruistic these men might be; and because we began earlier in the Anglo-Saxon countries, and because in that respect and in the development of that idea we have the advantage of 200 years of education in self-government, we unreasonably grace ourselves with a superiority in the matter of the knowledge of government which only circumstances have given us. Now we have arrived at a stage when the attention of the world is being directed toward the tropics, and along with this attention comes the movement towards popular government. It has already fallen to the lot of the people of the United States, who have struggled along the road to popular government, have at times fallen down and then have picked themselves up again, to aid some of the countries who have not had that experience in coming to the enjoyment and benefits of popular government. The Island of Cuba established as a Republic four years ago made such rapid progress in four years as almost to intoxicate those of us who believed in popular government. It was very like the growth of a tropical plant that needed to be cut back in order that the stem or stalk might gain in strength. It was perhaps necessary that this people should have, and sad as it was, a warning that the foundations upon which popular self-government must be laid, must be broad and solid rather than high and conspicuous. It is sad to me to be called to this Island, and still sadder to my chief, President Roosevelt, who was so identified with the liberation of this Island, to be here at a time of stumble [sic] in the progress toward popular self-government of this people. But however that may be, it has given us the opportunity which I now am glad to be able to take, to assure you in the name of President Roosevelt and the American people, we are here only to help you on. With our arm under your arm on the path to wonderful progress that you have traveled, we shall, I am confident, be again able to point with pride to the fact that the United States is not an exploiting nation but only has that deep sympathy with the progress of popular government as to be willing to expend its blood and treasure in making the spread of such government in the world successful. Now, following the usual course of the Anglo-Saxon which I have referred to as somewhat conceited and abrupt, perhaps you will pardon me if I invite your attention as an educated and intelligent audience to some of the difficulties of your people and of a possible method in meeting them. Your difficulty was this, that you were brought up under 15th and 16th century ideas of government, the government of one man or a few men, and that you were taught to look to somebody else for the responsibility of government. You exercised only the function of criticism (and in the old days that criticism had to be restrained in the face of government) and the most of your people, especially those of the educated and wealthy classes, trained themselves to occupy a position not of indifference but to inactivity with reference to political and governmental matters. Now it seems to me I find here a relic, although the reasons for it have disappeared, of that condition, and I find that the law is committed to one class, that the medicine is left to another, that the commercial interests are left to a third class, and that the political matters are left to a fourth class, and that the three classes, other than the political class lean back through the influences of past associations, watch with intense interest, but I fear with not a great deal of influence on what is done by the government. I venture to suggest that if the other classes do not take an active part and insist on exerting their influence in politics the question naturally arises, what was the necessity of changing your form of government at all? The theory of popular government is that all classes shall exercise decided political influence. Now I have discovered (one thinks he learns a great deal in a few days and it is quite characteristic of the Anglo-Saxon race that I should be talking to you in this way, but I must talk) it has seemed to me that your ideals are too high; I speak that with a qualification. An idea that is so high that it is beyond the reach of the real is not very useful. Soaring into the blue ethereal without any knowledge of the ground to which you must come is dangerous, because before you get through you are apt to strike the ground and the higher you get the more disastrous the fall. As the distinguished speaker of the day said as he closed his remarks (for that is what I think he said, if my limited knowledge of Spanish serves me) the hope of this country is in the generous and educated youth who are graduating from this and other institutions. Now I do not want to say anything that is going to jar or make uncomfortable the young men going forward into life to become useful, and yet I must speak the truth. There are one or two traditions that still persist in this civilization, the first of which is that the learned professions are the only pursuits worthy of the graduates of University and educated men. This is a great mistake. In the first place a University education is not an obstruction to success in commercial and mercantile life. It aids, if properly used. I am afraid that the young Cubans who are coming forward into life are not sufficiently infused with the mercantile spirit of which we have too much in America. What you need here among the Cubans is a desire to make money, to found great enterprises, and to carry on the prosperity of this beautiful Island and the young Cubans ought the most of them to begin in business. Every one knows your capacity and ability and there will be no trouble in forcing yourselves ahead in the next generation so that the banks and the commercial houses and the shipping interests of this country shall be in Cuban hands and not in the hands of foreigners. It is quite true that in order to help Cuba you must have foreign capital and the profound debt of gratitude this country owes to that great man, Tomás Estrada Palma, is that he realized more than any of the Cuban people the necessity of bringing foreign capital in here and convincing the world of the conservative nature of your government in order that foreign capital might depend on the security without which capital will not come. But the coming of foreign capital is not at all inconsistent with the gradual acquisition of capital by industrious, enterprising, intelligent, energetic, patriotic Cubans. The right of property and the motive for accumulation, next to the right of liberty, is the basis of all modern, successful civilization, and until you have a community of political influence and control which is effected by the conserving influence of property and property ownership, successful popular government is impossible. Therefore I urge upon you the young men who are going out into life today, who have shown excellence in their studies evidenced by these diplomas, that they devote their attention, if they have estates in the Island, to the betterment of those estates, and that others who have not estates, if they can get into the commercial houses and into commercial pursuits, do so, so that when twenty five years hence a sympathetic stranger comes here again he may not find the governing or political class, the commercial class, the class representing the sciences and the professions, all different and divided, so that they do not have the benefit of the mixture of all these classes who form that combination without which a successful republic is absolutely impossible—a safe, conservative, patriotic, self-sacrificing public opinion.

It gives me great pleasure, ladies and gentlemen, to have met you, and to have had the honor of saying this much to you, and I wish to thank the rector of the University and the faculty for giving me this opportunity.

I have only to say to you, "be not discouraged" as no one ever achieved a high ideal without failing two or three times, and the only way to make failures successes is to make these failures the vehicle of leading on to success, to take to your hearts the lesson that each stumble and each failure ought to teach, and the next time to avoid that particular danger and to move on toward success. Nothing worth having was ever planned without struggle and work and disappointment and failure. When every thing is smooth, when the winds blow the right way, and when you seem on the high road to success, then is the dangerous time. It is when you are humbled with a lesson taught from a disappointment that you are in the proper spirit to win success.

Viva The Republic of Cuba!

Taft Papers, in Manuscript Division, Library of Congress.

THE ROOT-TAKAHIRA AGREEMENT (1908)

Taft had established such a degree of rapport between Washington and Tokyo that Secretary Root's work was made almost routine in the furthering of friendship between the powers. The ranking Japanese officials had come to respect and trust the United States because of both the words and the attitude of the Secretary of War, and Root was able to add reassurances in consequence.

Imperial Japanese Embassy, Washington, November 30, 1908

THE EXCHANGE of views between us, which has taken place at the several interviews which I have recently had the honor of holding with you, has shown that Japan and the United States holding important outlying insular possessions in the region of the Pacific Ocean, the Governments of the two countries are animated by a common aim, policy, and intention in that region.

Believing that a frank avowal of that aim, policy, and intention would not only tend to strengthen the relations of friendship and good neighborhood, which have immemorially existed between Japan and the United States, but would materially contribute to the preservation of the general peace, the Imperial Government have authorized me to present to you an outline of their understanding of that common aim, policy, and intention:

1. It is the wish of the two Governments to encourage the free and peaceful development of their commerce on the Pacific Ocean.

2. The policy of both Governments, uninfluenced by any aggressive tendencies, is directed to the maintenance of the existing status quo in the region above

mentioned and to the defense of the principle of equal opportunity for commerce and industry in China.

3. They are accordingly firmly resolved reciprocally to respect the territorial possessions belonging to each other in said region.

4. They are also determined to preserve the common interest of all powers in China by supporting by all pacific means at their disposal the independence and integrity of China and the principle of equal opportunity for commerce and industry of all nations in that Empire.

5. Should any event occur threatening the status quo as above described or the principle of equal opportunity as above defined, it remains for the two Governments to communicate with each other in order to arrive at an understanding as to what measures they may consider it useful to take.

If the foregoing outline accords with the view of the Government of the United States, I shall be gratified to receive your confirmation. . . .

———

Papers Relating to the Foreign Relations of the United States, 1908, pp. 510-11.

CANADIAN RECIPROCITY TREATY (1911)

Believing as he did in the "economic man," friendly and free trade between the two English-speaking neighbors appealed to President Taft as a "natural" outcome of culture and geography. If he underestimated the power of special interests in the Senate as well as the insecurity among many Canadians about their political independence should the two nations become more economically connected, he did so because he professed to see far more good and very little harm arising from the treaty proposals.

SPECIAL MESSAGE ON CANADIAN RECIPROCITY
The White House, January 26, 1911

To the Senate and House of Representatives:

The guiding motive in seeking adjustment of Trade relations between two countries so situated geographically should be to give play to productive forces as far as practicable, regardless of political boundaries. While equivalency should be sought in an arrangement of this character, an exact balance of financial gain is neither imperative nor attainable. No yardstick can measure the benefits to the two peoples of this freer commercial intercourse and no trade agreement should be judged wholly by custom house statistics.

We have reached a stage in our own development that calls for a statesmanlike and broad view of our future economic status and its requirements. We have drawn upon our natural resources in such a way as to invite attention to their necessary limit. This has properly aroused effort to conserve them, to avoid their waste, and to restrict their use of our necessities. We have so increased in population and in our consumption of food products and the other necessities of life, hitherto supplied largely from our own country, that unless we materially increase our production we can see before us a change in our economic position, from that of a country selling to the world food and natural products of the farm and forest, to one consuming and importing them. Excluding cotton, which is exceptional, a radical change is already shown in our exports in the falling off in the amount of our agricultural products sold abroad and a corresponding marked increase in our manufactures exported.   A farsighted policy requires that if we can enlarge our supply of natural resources, and especially of food products and the necessities of life, without substantial injury to any of our producing and manufacturing classes, we should take steps to do so now. We have on the north of us a country contiguous to ours for three thousand miles, with natural resources of the same character as ours which have not been drawn upon as ours have been, and in the development of which the conditions as to wages and character of the wage earner and transportation to market differ but little from those prevailing with us. The difference is not greater than it is between different States of our own country or between different Provinces of the Dominion of Canada. Ought we not, then, to arrange a commercial agreement with Canada, if we can, by which we shall have direct access to her great supply of natural products without an obstructing or prohibitory tariff? This is not a violation of the protective principle, as that has been authoritatively announced by those who uphold it, because that principle does not call for a tariff between this country and one whose conditions as to production, population, and wages are so like ours, and when our common boundary line of three thousand miles in itself must make a radical distinction between our commercial treatment of Canada and of any other country.

The Dominion has greatly prospered. It has an active, aggressive, and intelligent people. They are coming to the parting of the ways. They must soon decide whether they are to regard themselves as isolated permanently from our markets by a perpetual wall or whether we are to be commercial friends. If we give them reason to take the former view, can we complain if they adopt methods denying access to certain of their natural resources except upon conditions quite unfavorable to us? A notable instance of such a possibility may be seen in the conditions surrounding the supply of pulp wood and the manufacture of print paper, for which we have made a conditional provision in the agreement, believed to be equitable. Should we not now, therefore, before their policy has become too crystallized and fixed for change, meet them in a spirit of real concession, facilitate commerce between the two countries, and thus greatly increase the natural resources available to our people?

I do not wish to hold out the prospect that the unrestricted interchange of food products will greatly and at once reduce their cost to the people of this country. Moreover, the present small amount of Canadian surplus for export as compared with that of our own production and consumption would make the reduction gradual. Excluding the element of transportation, the price of staple food products, especially of cereals, is much the same the world over, and the recent increase in price has been the result of a world-wide cause. But a source of supply as near as Canada would certainly help to prevent speculative fluctuations, would steady local price movements, and would postpone the effect of a further world increase in the price of leading commodities entering into the cost of living, if that be inevitable. . . .

My purpose in making a reciprocal trade agreement with Canada has been not only to obtain one which would be mutually advantageous to both countries, but one which also would be truly national in its scope as applied to our own country and would be of benefit to all sections. The currents of business and the transportation facilities that will be established forward and back across the border cannot but inure to the benefit of the boundary States. Some readjustments may be needed, but in a very short period the advantage of the free commercial exchange between communities separated only by short distances will strikingly manifest itself. That the broadening of the sources of food supplies, that the opening of the timber resources of the Dominion to our needs, that the addition to the supply of raw materials, will be limited to no particular section does not require demonstration. The same observation applies to the markets which the Dominion offers us in exchange. As an illustration, it has been found possible to obtain free entry into Canada for fresh fruits and vegetables—a matter of special value to the South and to the Pacific coast in disposing of their products in their season. It also has been practicable to obtain free entry for the cottonseed oil of the South—a most important product with a rapidly expanding consumption in the Dominion.

The entire foreign trade of Canada in the last fiscal year, 1910, was \$655,000,000. The imports were \$376,000,000, and of this amount the United States contributed more than \$233,000,000. The reduction in the duties imposed by Canada will largely increase this amount and give us even a larger share of her market than we now enjoy, great as that is.

The data accompanying the text of the trade agreement exhibit in detail the facts which are here set forth briefly and in outline only. They furnish full information on which the legislation recommended may be based. Action on the agreement submitted will not interfere with such revision of our own tariff on imports from all countries as Congress may decide to adopt.

Reciprocity with Canada must necessarily be chiefly confined in its effect on the cost of living to food and forest products. The question of the cost of clothing as affected by duty on textiles and their raw materials, so much mooted, is not within the scope of an agreement with Canada, because she raises comparatively few wool sheep, and her textile manufactures are unimportant.

This trade agreement, if entered into, will cement the friendly relations with the Dominion which have resulted from the satisfactory settlement of the controversies that have lasted for a century, and further promote good feeling between kindred peoples. It will extend the market for numerous products of the United States among the inhabitants of a prosperous neighboring country with an increasing population and an increasing purchasing power. It will deepen and widen the sources of food supply in contiguous territory, and will facilitate the movement and distribution of these foodstuffs.

The geographical proximity, the closer relation of blood, common sympathies, and identical moral and social ideas furnish very real and striking reasons why this agreement ought to be viewed from a high plane.

Since becoming a nation, Canada has been our good neighbor, immediately contiguous across a wide continent without artificial or natural barrier except navigable waters used in common.

She has cost us nothing in the way of preparations for defense against her possible assault, and she never will. She has sought to agree with us quickly when differences have disturbed our relations. She shares with us common traditions and aspirations. I feel I have correctly interpreted the wish of the American people by expressing, in the arrangement now submitted to Congress for its approval, their desire for a more intimate and cordial relationship with Canada. I therefore earnestly hope that the measure will be promptly enacted into law.

William Howard Taft, *Collected Works*, Vol. IV, pp. 105-10.

ARBITRATION TREATIES (1911)

The underlying premise of the treaties as Taft had them drafted was that advanced, civilized nations, sharing common values and historic bonds, must take the lead in demonstrating that no issue that might arise between them was not justiciable. In a sense Taft was quite alone in his outlook. He is to be all the more respected for such a conviction and the willingness to put it to the test. What made its rejection by the Senate distressful was that he deemed it to be the capstone of his presidency.

Article I. All differences hereafter arising between the High Contracting Parties, which it has not been possible to adjust by diplomacy, relating to international matters in which the High Contracting Parties are concerned by virtue of a claim of right made by one against the other under treaty or otherwise, and which are justiciable in their nature by reason of being susceptible of decision by the application of the principles of law or equity, shall be submitted to the Permanent Court of Arbitration established at The Hague by the Convention of October 18, 1907, or to some other arbitral tribunal, as shall [may] be decided in each case by special agreement, which special agreement shall provide for the organization of such tribunal if necessary, define the scope of the powers of the arbitrators, the question or questions at issue, and settle the terms of reference and the procedure thereunder. . . .

Article II. In each individual case the high contracting parties, before appealing to the Permanent Court of Arbitration, shall conclude a special agreement defining clearly the matter in dispute, the scope of the powers of the arbitrators, and the periods to be fixed for the formation of the arbitral tribunal and the several stages of the procedure.

It is understood that on the part of the United States such special agreements will be made by the President of the United States, by and with the advice and consent of the Senate, and on the part of France they will be subject to the procedure required by the constitutional laws of France.

Article III. The present convention shall be ratified by the President of the United States of America, by and with the advice and and consent of the Senate thereof; it shall become effective on the day of such ratification, and shall remain in force for a period of five years thereafter. . . .

Senate Document No. 476, 62nd Congress, 2nd Session (6176), pp. 2-6.

DOLLAR DIPLOMACY (1912)

Taft and his administration of the Department of State launched a
new phase in American foreign policy by seeking to influence the political stability of the nations of Central America by encouraging and
protecting private capitalist investments by the major eastern banking
houses. The policy enjoyed limited success despite Taft's intention of
shoring up these nations politically by means of financial assistance.

   . . . The diplomacy of the present administration has
sought to respond to modern ideas of commercial intercourse. This policy has been characterized as substituting
dollars for bullets. It is one that appeals alike to idealistic
humanitarian sentiments, to the dictates of sound policy
and strategy, and to legitimate commercial aims. It is an
effort frankly directed to the increase of American trade
upon the axiomatic principle that the Government of the
United States shall extend all proper support to every legitimate and beneficial American enterprise abroad. How
great have been the results of this diplomacy, coupled with
the maximum and minimum provision of the tariff law, will
be seen by some consideration of the wonderful increase in
the export trade of the United States. Because modern
diplomacy is commercial, there has been a disposition in
some quarters to attribute to it none but materialistic aims.
How strikingly erroneous is such an impression may be
seen from a study of the results by which the diplomacy of
the United States can be judged. . . .

   In Central America the aim has been to help such countries as Nicaragua and Honduras to help themselves. They
are the immediate beneficiaries. The national benefit to
the United States is two-fold. First, it is obvious that the

Monroe doctrine is more vital in the neighborhood of the Panama Canal and the zone of the Caribbean than anywhere else. There, too, the maintenance of that doctrine falls most heavily upon the United States. It is therefore essential that the countries within that sphere shall be removed from the jeopardy involved by heavy foreign debt and chaotic national finances and from the ever-present danger of international complications due to disorder at home. Hence the United States has been glad to encourage and support American bankers who were willing to lend a helping hand to the financial rehabilitation of such countries because this financial rehabilitation and the protection of their customhouses from being the prey of would-be dictators would remove at one stroke the menace of foreign creditors and the menace of revolutionary disorder.

The second advantage to the United States is one affecting chiefly all the southern and Gulf ports and the business and industry of the South. The Republics of Central America and the Caribbean possess great natural wealth. They need only a measure of stability and the means of financial regeneration to enter upon an era of peace and prosperity, bringing profit and happiness to themselves and at the same time creating conditions sure to lead to a flourishing interchange of trade with this country.

I wish to call your especial attention to the recent occurrences in Nicaragua, for I believe the terrible events recorded there during the revolution of the past summer— the useless loss of life, the devastation of property, the bombardment of defenseless cities, the killing and wounding of women and children, the torturing of noncombatants to exact contributions, and the suffering of thousands of human beings—might have been averted had the Department of State, through approval of the loan convention by the Senate, been permitted to carry out its now well-developed policy of encouraging the extending of financial aid to weak Central American States with the primary objects of avoiding just such revolutions by assisting those Republics to rehabilitate their finances, to establish their currency on a stable basis, to remove the customhouses from the danger of revolutions by arranging for their secure administration, and to establish reliable banks.

During this last revolution in Nicaragua, the Government of that Republic having admitted its inability to protect American life and property against acts of sheer lawlessness on the part of the malcontents, and having requested this Government to assume that office, it became necessary to land over 2,000 marines and bluejackets in Nicaragua. Owing to their presence the constituted Government of Nicaragua was free to devote its attention wholly to its internal troubles, and was thus enabled to stamp out the rebellion in a short space of time. When the Red Cross supplies sent to Granada had been exhausted, 8,000 persons having been given food in one day upon the arrival of the American forces, our men supplied other unfortunate, needy Nicaraguans from their own haversacks. I wish to congratulate the officers and men of the United States Navy and Marine Corps who took part in reestablishing order in Nicaragua upon their splendid conduct, and to record with sorrow the death of seven American marines and bluejackets. Since the reestablishment of peace and order, elections have been held amid conditions of quiet and tranquility. Nearly all the

American marines have now been withdrawn. The country should soon be on the road to recovery. The only apparent danger now threatening Nicaragua arises from the shortage of funds. Although American bankers have already rendered assistance, they may naturally be loathe to advance a loan adequate to set the country upon its feet without the support of some such conventions as that of June, 1911, upon which the Senate has not yet acted. . . .

Message of the President of the United States on Our Foreign Relations, Communicated to the Two Houses of Congress, December 3, 1912 (Washington, 1912), pp. 7-8, 10-11.

Taft, *Collected Works*, Vol. IV, pp. 288, 290-292.

The Warrant From History (1915)

The founding document of the League To Enforce Peace was so termed. It is disarming in its simplicity, and one that requires of its readers and/or supporters no explication. Of course it did not pretend to be a covenant or a treaty or a protocol. It was more like an announcement, better still, a declaration, of a cause to which men might rally.

PROPOSALS

We believe it to be desirable for the United States to join a league of nations binding the signatories to the following:

First: All justiciable questions arising between the signatory powers, not settled by negotiation, shall, subject to the limitations of treaties, be submitted to a judicial tribunal for hearing and judgment, both upon the merits and upon any issue as to its jurisdiction of the question.

Second: All other questions arising between the signatories and not settled by negotiation shall be submitted to a council of conciliation for hearing, consideration and recommendation.

Third: The signatory powers shall jointly use forthwith both their economic and military forces against any one of their number that goes to war, or commits acts of hostility, against another of the signatories before any question arising shall be submitted as provided in the foregoing.

Fourth: Conferences between the signatory powers shall be held from time to time to formulate and codify rules of international law, which, unless some signatory shall signify its dissent within a stated period, shall thereafter govern in the decisions of the Judicial Tribunal mentioned in Article One.

Taft, *Collected Works*, Vol. VII, pp. 3-4.

SELF-DETERMINATION (1919)

One of the thorniest problems which thrust itself into public discourse and diplomatic negotiations was the Wilsonian principle of self-determination of nations. Once in effect it would bring down some mighty empires. Taft believed in self-determination but was fully alive to the difficulty of implementing it to the satisfaction of all ethnic or linguistic groups. He was therefore at pains to warn the conquered and the conquerors alike to proceed slowly and cautiously in assessing the several different situations and to seek to resolve conflicting demands that had already arisen.

The task of the League of Nations called to decide the terms of peace will be as huge as that of the war which the peace will end. The issues as to Alsace-Lorraine, the Trentino and Trieste will be simple as compared with the Czecho-Slovak and Jugo-Slav questions. The restrictions of the Turkish domain, the protection and freedom of Armenia, the Balkan boundaries and the government of Albania will try the ingenuity of statesmen in working out a just result. Above all in difficulty will be the settlement of the questions as to Russia. Shall it be a confederation of States like ours, or shall they be independent? Who shall determine this?

"Let the people themselves decide," it is said. Every one agrees that this general rule should prevail in post-war arrangements. But how large or how small shall the unit of a people for such decision be? Shall units be racial or geographical? Suppose a people as small in number as the Belfast Orangemen compared with the whole population of Ireland insists on a separate government, though geography, trade conditions and every consideration but religious difference and tradition require that the whole island be under one Government?

It becomes apparent at once that the general principle of popular rule is not a panacea and that many issues will have to be settled by the Congress of Nations, according to expedient and practical justice, over the objection of some part of the people affected. The result will illustrate the inherent error in the frequent assumption that a Government by the people is a Government in which that which is done is the will of each one. A practical Government by the people is a Government by a majority of the voters. The rest of the people must yield their will to the will of this majority. However, in the purest democracy, the voters are not a half of the population, and the prevailing majority is usually not more than 20 per cent of all. The guide of the popular will is still less helpful when the issue is the fixing of the proper self-governing unit. In the intoxicating fumes of a new freedom, municipal Councils in Russia declared themselves independent governments. Should Lithuania, Estonia, the Ukraine and Great Russia be separate entities? This cannot be certainly and properly determined by a plebiscite of the population of the particular district, if its relation to the neighboring communities or to Russia as a whole make it best for all concerned that they be united. More than this, an ignorant people without the slightest experience in the restraints necessary in successful self-government and subject to the wildest imaginings under the insidious demagoguery of venal leaders may well not know what is best for them.

Thus, flowing phrases as to liberty and the rule of the people do not offer a complete solution for all the problems which the world's peacemakers will face. Still, if we can make the adjustment to depend on just provision for the welfare of the peoples affected instead of on the greed of the parties, we shall secure an enormous advance over past international settlements.

Taft, *Collected Works*, Vol. VII, pp. 123-24.

SENATOR LODGE ON THE LEAGUE OF NATIONS (1919)

Taft was keen to include in his campaign for acceptance of the basic idea of a league or association of nations as many ranking Republicans as possible. He derived both personal and political pleasure by referencing Senator Lodge's public support of the kind of league Taft favored, one that presupposed the critical role of the great powers. If Lodge in his address to the Senate was not really in support of President Wilson's position, Taft was eager to exploit what could be discerned in the Senator's words that favored the fundamentals of international cooperation with the United States an active participant.

Senator Lodge's speech in the Senate on the twenty-first of this month was the best yet made on the aims of the Allies and the elements of a satisfactory treaty of peace. It was comprehensive and accurate, lucid and forcible, felicitous in phrase and elevated in tone. It was in the senator's best style, and that is a high standard.

Its great merit is in its broad vision of the real purposes of the the United States and her present obligation. The senator summarizes certain objections to the general League of Nations. These are, as lawyers would say, *obiter dicta* in this speech, because he now asks a postponement of that subject matter, not its rejection on its merits.

There are those who minimize the burden the United States should assume in execution of this peace; they deny that she should share it with her Allies. Mr. Lodge is not one of those. He is not a little American. He does not recur to the farewell address of Washington and the phrase, "entangling alliances," enjoined by Jefferson in order to employ them narrowly to limit the responsibilities of the United States, now that it has become the most powerful nation in the world.

In his address he said: "We went to war to save civilization. For this mighty purpose we have sacrificed thousands of American lives and spent billions of American treasure. We cannot, therefore, leave the work half done. We are as much bound, not merely by interests and every consideration for a safe future, but by honor and self-respect, to see that the terms of peace are carried out, as we were to fulfill our great determination that the armies of Germany should be defeated in the field. We cannot halt or turn back now. We must do our share to carry out the peace as we have done our share to win the war, of which the peace is an integral part. We must do our share in the occupation of German territory which will be held as security for the indemnities to be paid by Germany. We cannot escape doing our part in aiding the peoples to whom we have helped to give freedom and independence in establishing themselves with ordered governments, for in no other way can we erect the barriers which are essential to prevent another outbreak by Germany upon the world. We cannot leave the Jugo-Slavs, the Czecho-Slovaks and the Poles, the Lithuanians and the other states which we hope to see formed and marching upon the path of progress and development, unaided and alone."

He says that the United States is obliged to aid Russia in rising from the chaos and disorder which has come upon her to the place which she ought to occupy in the family of nations; that the object of the Russian Bolsheviki has been to destroy their fellow citizens and every element which was necessary to a social fabric under which men could live and prosper while they themselves profit in money and in power from the ruin they have wrought; that they indulged in murder and massacre, destroyed property and all the instruments of industry, and the unhappy and ignorant people of Russia, in whose name they undertook to act, are today suffering from famine and disease, and are in a worse condition than they were in the days of the Romanoffs; that if Russian anarchy should be permitted to spread through western civilization, that civilization would fall; that we cannot leave Russia lying helpless and breathing out infection on the world; and that it would be discreditable to the United States if we failed to recognize our duty to her.

The Senator's speech was delivered to establish the necessity for postponing the consideration by the conference of five of the fourteen points of the President's message of January 8, referring to secret diplomacy, to freedom of navigation and the seas, to the removal of economic barriers, to the reduction of armament, and to the central League of Nations.

It must be admitted the Senator's argument for a postponement of these questions to an adjourned conference has weight. It may be that in the immediate settlement of them is to be found a means of solving difficulties in agreement upon specific terms of peace, of which neither the Senator nor we are advised.

A stipulation that the five Allies dictating this treaty should not make any treaty as between themselves inconsistent with the purpose of the great treaty and should make no secret treaties at all, may well strengthen mutual confidence in the good faith of all in the main treaty.

The general reduction of armaments of all nations does not immediately concern the peace in the sphere of war, provided Germany's teeth are effectively drawn.

The provision against economic barriers is a general question of world trade, the immediate settlement of which does not, on the surface, seem essential to the adjustment of the purposes of the nations in winning this war. The sub-currents of selfish purpose in respect to trade, however, may require a preliminary settlement of such a general principle as the best basis for adjusting special interests.

The freedom of the seas in time of war is a very general issue, postponement of which to the adjourned conference would hardly interfere with a satisfactory peace settlement for the present.

What should be emphasized, however, and what Senator Lodge brings out with force of argument that cannot be met, is the fact that we now have a league of nations—the United States, England, France, Italy and Japan—whose obligations in respect to securing the results of the war in Europe are equal. They are dictating this peace. The treaty will not enforce itself.

Unless we stamp out the poisonous infection of Russian Bolshevism and prevent its spread throughout the countries of Europe, we shall only substitute anarchy, chaos and plundering, murderous violence for imperial despotism.

We can only achieve these results by continuance of this existing league of Great Powers. Of this Senator Lodge's great address is a demonstration.

Taft, *Collected Works*, Vol. VII, pp. 161-64.

CRITICISM SHOULD BE CONSTRUCTIVE (1919)

The ex-President has often been characterized as a maladroit politician. His plea for constructive criticism of the Wilsonian proposal for a League of Nations was in fact an adroit move on his part. Not only does he once again pay deference to Senator Lodge's understanding of the League, but he urges all critics to scrutinize the language and intent of the President's proposals, asking for helpful suggestions as how to re-order the post-war world.

Objections to a general League of Nations are numerous. Senator Borah makes merry over it. The funny column of the *Evening Sun* is filled with hypotheses of its operation and its absurd results. Mr.Lodge and Mr. Knox treat the proposal with more deference. Mr. Lodge in a speech at the dinner of the League to Enforce Peace in May, 1916, advocated the use of force to support an international tribunal's judgment. Since that time he has changed his mind, but in his last speech he appreciates the seriousness of the proposal sufficiently to discuss in more detail the plan of the League. Mr. Knox has favored treaties of universal arbitration of justiciable questions and therefore has also a past to observe.

The force and weight of objections to the League should be gathered first from the attitude of mind of the objector. If he is content to dispose of the matter on the ground that the idea is an old one and has never been realized, we are not likely to have useful help from him. One who does not hope that the great war has changed the feeling of the peoples of the world toward war so that they are willing to bind themselves to a world policy of peace as they never were before will certainly not entertain the plea of the League with patience. He must be waked up before he will give it his consideration. One who has no sense of responsibility about future world peace, but is anxious to return to domestic business and politics, is equally beyond reach.

It is only from those who appreciate our great opportunity in the dreadful results of this war to arouse all peoples to the wisdom of uniting the major force of the world to prevent their recurrence that we can have sympathetic discussion and constructive thought. The proposal of a league of nations should not be flouted because the members of the Senate are justifiably indignant over the way in which the President has ignored them and ignored Congress in this matter. When he returns with a treaty providing for some kind of a league of nations to maintain peace, the people are unlikely to be interested in the personal soreness of the Senate or to accept that as any factor in judging the treaty. The Democrats of the Senate, with only one or two exceptions, will approve what the President submits. If the Republicans who object to the League are numerous enough to defeat the treaty they will have to decide whether their objection is really so weighty and sincere that they wish to furnish it as an issue to the President and his party in the next campaign. The pressure of the popular desire will be to have immediate peace. The party which delays that must have a strong case.

The League of Nations is very strong with the peoples of Europe. It is growing stronger here. Organized labor has approved it. It is going to attract the mass of wage-earners and the plain people as it has abroad. With the President and the Democratic party behind it, Republican objectors who manifest no constructive desire to create machinery to keep the peace, but depend wholly as of old on armament and troops to settle difficulties, will not be heard with favor. The contemptuous skepticism of the Senate cloakroom, the cheap sarcasms of "the old diplomatic and senatorial band," the manifest spirit of "how not to do it," will be very poor weapons with which to combat an idealistic campaign for a definite plan for permanent peace and democracy.

The next presidential campaign promises well for the Republican party if that party, through its congressional representatives, does nothing to change the present trend. But if enough Republican senators attempt to defeat or hold up the treaty of peace because it makes the United States a member of a League of Nations to maintain peace they will seriously endanger the chance of Republican success.

The Senators who discuss any plan for a League should show their interest, not by knocking it out with one blow, but by suggesting changes in it which would be more practical than the ideals proposed and would still serve the general purpose. They should make their consideration hopeful and optimistic by searching for alternative details of method which might avoid the objections they conceive. If any of the critics of the League in the Senate, or out of it, have given such evidence of their sympathetic interest in the project and its purpose, it has not been brought to our knowledge. The whole tone of the objectors has been pessimistic. Running through all their attacks is the cynical assumption that the great war has made no difference in the attitude and duty of the peoples of the world toward war and peace, except that for the time it has injured the power of Germany to make further trouble. They, in effect, advocate the retirement of the United States to its shell of isolation, to reappear again only when the war-making proclivities of any nation, Germany, or any other country, shall threaten the interests of the United States. This is the gospel of despair and national selfishness.

The possibility of a breach of national faith may be pointed out as a weakness of the League. If so, it is inherent in every treaty, the value and utility of which must ultimately rest in the honor of the nations making it. The more responsible the nations the greater their power of performance, the keener their appreciation of their honor, the clearer their perception of the value to themselves and the world of maintaining the treaty, the greater the certainty that the treaty will live and effect its purpose.

Taft, *Collected Works*, Vol. VII, pp. 182-84.

To Make Peace Secure (1919)

In his address at the Methodist Church in Augusta, Georgia, Taft delivered one of his most powerful and persuasive statements in support of world order. It was thorough, explanatory, well-reasoned, and utterly sincere. Rereading his remarks demonstrates beyond doubt that he had committed himself in a "come what may" fashion to the principles of law and order as the means to peace and prosperity for a world weary of death and destruction. He was convinced he knew what the American people wanted of both the President and the Senate, and saw himself standing squarely with the people. In a word William Howard Taft was a true-blue Progressive when it came to promoting the cause of the will of the people.

I favor the obligation on the part of all the nations to use their military force to maintain the covenants of the League. That was a feature of the plan of the League to Enforce Peace. I do not think it is clearly set forth in the present Covenant. The nearer it comes to that the more satisfactory it is to me, and the more effective that League will become. The burden of carrying on war, which has been held up as a reason for not entering the League, is one entirely removed by the certainty of cooperation of the nations. The usefulness of such a league is far greater in its warning and restraining effect upon reckless nations willing to begin war than even in its actual suppression of war. It is vastly more economical on our part to agree that, should occasion arise, we will contribute economic and military pressure to suppress war than it is to refuse such an agreement and then be drawn into a war like the one we have just passed through, leaving an indebtedness of twenty-five billions, a war that would have been avoided by the knowledge on the part of Germany and Austria that aggression would array the whole world against them. The arguments that Senator Borah advances in this regard are arguments that are the figments of his imagination. The very object of the League is to prevent war, not to fight little wars, and the clearer the obligation to exert economic pressure and military force against the aggressor, the greater the improbability that wars will come. Instead of being a source of increased expense, the League will greatly reduce expenses to the government of the Untied States, first, in reducing armaments, and second, in reducing the number of the wars into which it is likely to be drawn.

If the provisions I have mentioned were limited to the members of the League they would lack comprehensiveness in preserving world peace, because it may be some time before two-thirds of the Body of Delegates shall conclude that it is wise to admit to permanent membership in the League countries like Germany, Austria, Turkey or Bulgaria, or countries with no sense of responsibility and so weak in police power and self-restraint as not to be able to perform the covenants of the League. To correct what otherwise would be a defect in the constitution of the League, there is a declaration that the League is interested in war between any countries whether members of the League or not, and will take such action as the peace of the world may require in order to prevent injury from such a war.

The four great steps to secure peace are, first, reduction of armament; second, union against conquest by arms; third, peaceful settlements of differences and a covenant not to begin war until every effort has been made to secure such peaceful settlement, together with a world boycott of the outlaw nation and the exercise of military compulsion, if necessary; and finally, fourth, the inhibition of all secret treaties and an enforcement of open diplomacy. Nothing like it has heretofore been attempted in the history of the world. The problem of German peace has forced it. . . .

We have fourteen nations, seven of them being the nations who won the war with Germany, agreeing through their representatives at Paris upon these steps. The question now is whether the Senate of the United States is to destroy the possibility of this advance in the civilization of the world by its vote against the action of the President and against what I verily believe to be the opinion of the majority of the people of the United States. I would unhesitatingly vote for the Covenant just as it was unanimously reported by the committee of representatives of the fourteen countries engaged in drafting the treaty. I am hopeful, however, that the fears of some, who conscientiously favor the treaty, as to certain possibilities of danger may be removed by more express limitation. The treaty is in process of amendment now and any clarifying amendments should be welcomed in order, if possible, to secure ratification. I believe the President and the Commission have a sense of duty in this regard and that we may look for amendments of this character.

What are the objections of the League? They are, first, that the United States has gotten along so well since the beginning without being drawn into the politics of the outside world that it ought to keep out of them and ought not to involve itself in a league of nations. This opinion, I think we may say, is confined to a small body of persons represented by Senators Borah, Reed and Poindexter. If there are others who take this position in the Senate, their names do not occur to me. All the other members of the Senate who have objected to this covenant have averred that they are in favor of a league of nations to secure peace. If they are, they are in favor of something that binds the United States to some kind of an obligation to help in the preservation of peace. A league of nations means something that binds one nation to another in respect to certain obligations. That is the etymological derivation of the word and that is its actual meaning. If they are therefore in favor of a league of nations, they have, by that fact, admitted the necessity of departing from the traditional policy of the United States to enter into no alliances with foreign nations, because a league is an alliance, and, as a league contains obligations, it must entangle the United States to the extent at least of the performance of those obligations.

We cannot avoid being affected by international quarrels in Europe. It is economical for us to unite with the other countries to maintain peace instead of waiting until we are driven into war and then making a superhuman effort to defend ourselves against a war that has meantime grown into enormous proportions because of our failure, and that of the other nations of the world to suppress it in its inception. . . .

The Executive Council has no power to fix the obligation. It does not determine conclusively for any member of the League any fact upon which the obligation of that member becomes immediate. Its duties are executive in the sense that it acquires all the necessary information, follows closely matters with which the League has to do and takes action in the sense of making a recommendation to the various Powers as to how the difficulties shall be met. It furnishes a means by which the Powers confer together in order that they may agree upon joint action; but in no sense is any power delegated to it to declare war, to wage war, to declare a boycott, to limit armament or to force arbitration.

The only two things which it does, things that can be said in any way to be binding on nations are, first, not to increase the limit of armament to which a nation has agreed to confine itself after full consideration, and, second (where jurisdiction is not taken from it by reference to the Body of Delegates) if it can act unanimously, to make a report of settlement of a difficulty such that if the defendant nation complies with it, the plaintiff nation may not begin war to get more. It may propose measures to the members of the League by which they can carry out its recommendations of settlement, but it does not decide upon those measures and it is left to the members of the League to agree whether they desire to use force to carry out recommendations or not. In every other respect its action is advisory and of a recommending character.

Still less can there be said to be sovereign authority delegated to the Body of Delegates. The Body of Delegates selects the four countries whose representatives are to enter the Executive Council. It elects, by two-thirds vote, new members to the League after they have shown themselves able to fulfill the covenants of the League. It may be substituted as a mediating body and a body to recommend settlement in place of the Executive Council. It may also advise the reconsideration by members of the League of treaties which have become inapplicable to international conditions and which may endanger the peace of the world. This is all.

It is impossible, therefore, for one looking through the Covenant, without a determined purpose to formulate objections to it, to find any transfer of sovereignty to the Executive Council or the Body of Delegates. The whole theory of the Covenant is that the nations are to act together under obligations of the Covenant, that they are to come to an agreement, through these two bodies, but that the action to be taken is to be determined by each nation on its conscience under its agreement, and that when the action is to be taken it is to be taken by that nation in accord with its constitution.

Taft, *Collected Works*, Vol. VII, pp. 267-70.

The Victory Program (1918)

Adopted at a meeting of the Executive Committee, held in New York, November 23, 1918, as the official platform of the League to Enforce Peace, this statement superseded the proposals adopted by the League in 1915. The influence of Taft on the new document is readily apparent with regard to the procedure for dealing with justiciable issues as well as a call for a Council of Conciliation to resolve questions nonjusticiable in character.

The war now happily brought to a close has been above all a war to end war, but in order to ensure the fruits of victory and to prevent the recurrence of such a catastrophe there should be formed a League of Free Nations, as universal as possible, based upon treaty and pledged that the security of each state shall rest upon the strength of the whole. The initiating nucleus of the membership of the League should be the nations associated as belligerents in winning the war.

The League should aim at promoting the liberty, progress, and fair economic opportunity of all nations, and the orderly development of the world.

It should ensure peace by eliminating causes of dissension, by deciding controversies by peaceable means, and by uniting the potential force of all the members as a standing menace against any nation that seeks to upset the peace of the world.

The advantages of membership in the League, both economically and from the point of view of security, should be so clear that all nations will desire to be members of it.

For this purpose it is necessary to create—

1. For the decision of justiciable questions, an impartial tribunal whose jurisdiction shall not depend upon the assent of the parties to the controversy; provision to be made for enforcing its decisions.

2. For questions that are not justiciable in their character, a Council of Conciliation, as a mediator, which shall hear, consider, and make recommendations; and failing acquiescence by the parties concerned, the League shall determine what action, if any, shall be taken.

3. An administrative organization for the conduct of affairs of common interest, the protection and care of backward regions and internationalized places, and such matters as have been jointly administered before and during the war. We hold that this object must be attained by methods and through machinery that will ensure both stability and progress; preventing, on the one hand, any crystallization of the *status quo* that will defeat the forces of healthy growth and changes, and providing, on the other hand, a way by which progress can be secured and necessary change effected without recourse to war.

4. A representative Congress to formulate and codify rules of international law, to inspect the work of the administrative bodies and to consider any matter affecting the tranquility of the world or the progress or betterment of human relations. Its deliberations should be public.

5. An Executive Body, able to speak with authority in the name of the nations represented, and to act in case the peace of the world is endangered.

The representation of the different nations in the organs of the League should be in proportion to the responsibilities and obligations they assume. The rules of international law should not be defeated for lack of unanimity.

Taft, *Collected Works*, Vol. VII, pp. 5-6.

INDEX

A

Addyston Pipe and Steel case (1898), 22

Adee, Alvey A., 62–63, 67, 69–70

Aguinaldo, Emilio, 30–31

Alaska, 1, 18, 108

American Arbitration and Peace League, 80

American Peace Society, 85–86

American Society for the Judicial Settlement of International Disputes, 90

American Society of International Law, 87

arbitration: treaties of, 81, 86–89, 101; treaties of with Britain and France (1911), 64, 80, 82, 85, 103, 118; wording of 1911 treaties of, 143–44

Arthur, Chester A., 5, 14

Asquith, Herbert, 99

Atkinson, Frederick W., 34

B

Bacon, Robert, 42–43

balance of power, 28, 46–48, 115, 126

Barrett, John, 64

Beers, Henry, A., 7

Bering Sea case (1891), 18–19

Beveridge, Albert, 3

Borah, William, 96–97, 162, 164

Borden, Robert, 80

Bryan, William Jennings, 16

Bryce, James, 82, 101, 107

C

Canada: Alaskan boundary dispute with, 37, 108; reciprocity treaty with, 64, 77–80, 118; text of reciprocity treaty with, 137–42

Caribbean basin, U.S. commerce with, 63–64, 67–70, 145–46

Carnegie, Andrew, 2, 81

Cecil, Robert, 117

China: Open Door policy and, 28–29, 51–52, 64, 74; Taft's presidency and, 74–77; trade with, 28–29, 37, 41, 51–53

Costa Rica, boundary of, 116

Cuba, 40–44, 94, 128–34

D

Debs, Eugene V., 21

Diaz, Porfirio, 71–73

disarmament, 95, 100, 102

dollar diplomacy, 53, 61, 65, 67–70, 72, 74–76

Dominican Republic, 65, 69–70

E

Eliot, George, 7

Estrada, Juan, 66–68

evolution, 2

expansion, post-Civil War American, 1–3, 27, 74

F

Far East, U.S. commerce with, 63, 74–76. See also under China

Foraker, Joseph B., 14, 17

Fourteen Points, 99–100, 156–57

G

Geofrey v. Riggs, 94

Germany, war debt of, 116

H

Harding, Warren G., 115

Harrison, Benjamin, 17, 20

Havana, University of, text of Taft's address at, 128–34

Hay, John, 19, 28–29, 52

Hayashi, Tadasu, 49–50

Holt, Henry, 90–91

Honduras, 69

Howland, William B., 90

Huerta, Victoriano, 73

Hughes, Charles Evans, 117

Huntington-Wilson, Francis M., 61–62, 67–70

I

Influence of Sea Power on History, The (Mahan), 3

international law, 8–9, 19, 86–87, 103, 115

Introduction to the Study of International Law, An (Woolsey), 7–9

J

Japan, 45–52, 54, 118; texts of U.S. agreements with, 126–27, 135–36

Jay's Treaty, 94

Jusserand, Jules, 82

K

Katsura, Taro, 46–47, 51, 126–27

Knox, Philander C., 61–63, 66, 70, 75–76, 78, 82; and Versailles Treaty, 109, 157

Korea, 47, 126–27

L

Lake Mohonk conferences, 86

Laurier, Wilfred, 78

League of Nations, 89, 98–104, 109–10, 117–18, 151–68

League to Enforce Peace, 90–91, 100, 106; Taft and, 44, 92–96, 103, 163, 169; "Victory Program" of, 169–70; "Warrant from History" of, 149–50

Leo XIII (pope), 36

Lloyd George, David, 99, 116

Lodge, Henry Cabot, 19, 103–7, 109, 154–57

Long, John Davis, 23

Lowell, A. Lawrence, 91, 101

M

MacArthur, Arthur, 24, 31

Mahan, Alfred Thayer, 3, 73

Manchuria, 75–76, 118

Marburg, Theodore, 90–91

McKinley, William, 20, 22–23, 29–30, 32

McKinley Tariff, 19

Mexico, 70–73

Miller, W.H., 19

Monroe Doctrine, 59, 65–66, 82, 102, 146

Moores & Company v. Bricklayers Union No. 1 (1890), 16–17

N

nation building, 31–33

Nicaragua, 66–69, 146–48

O

Open Door policy, 28–29, 51–52, 54, 64, 74–75

P

Palma, Estrada Tomás, 41-42, 132

Panama, boundary of, 116

Panama Canal, 38–40, 146

peace, 80, 164–65; enforcement of, 81, 91–92, 96–97, 99–100, 105–6

Permanent Court of Arbitration, 143

Permanent Court of International Justice, 117

Platt Amendment, 41–42

Phelan, In re: (1894), 21–22

Philippines: American acquisition of, 3, 23; independence movement in, 30–31; Roman Catholic Church in, 34–36; as U.S. possession, 23, 40–41, 46–4 7, 126; William Howard Taft's governorship of, 23–24, 29–34, 37

popular government, 129–33, 150-51

Popular Government (Taft), 87

Populism, 15–16

President and His Powers, The (Taft), 88–89

property, private, 12, 16, 22, 34, 133

Pullman strike (1894), 16, 21

R

Reed, Thomas, 19, 166

religion, freedom of, 98

Rizal, José, 30, 35

Roosevelt, Theodore: as ex-President, 79, 96–97, 103, 107–9; and the Monroe Doctrine, 65–66; as President, 35, 37, 42, 46–48, 54, 61; Taft and, 19–20, 38, 45, 88

Root, Elihu, 23, 103–4, 117, 135

Root-Takahira agreement, 54; text of, 135–36

Russell, W.W., 70

Russia, 53, 75–76, 155–57

Russo-Japanese War, 45–47

S

self-determination (of peoples), 98–100; text of Taft's statement on, 150–52

Sherman Anti-Trust Act, 22

Social Darwinism, 9–10, 12, 60

Straight, Willard, 53, 75

Sumner, William Graham, 7–10, 12,

60

Supreme Court, U.S., 93, 102; Taft as chief justice of, 115–17

T

Taft, Alphonso, 4–6, 12–13, 53

Taft, Helen "Nellie" Herron (Mrs. William Howard), 6, 14–15, 18–20, 23–24

Taft, Horace, 23

Taft, Louise Torrey (Mrs. Alphonso), 4–6

Taft, William Howard: family background and upbringing of, 1, 4–6, 12, 118; education of, 6–12, 118; early political career of, 13–16; as jurist, 4, 16–17, 20–22, 94, 115–17; as solicitor general, 17–20; as civil governor of the Philippines, 3, 16, 22–24, 29–37; as secretary of war, 37–40, 42–54, 126–38; as interim governor of Cuba, 43–44, 128–34; diplomatic experience of, 3–4, 27, 44–45, 48–54, 59–60, 118; as President, 59–82, 85, 118, 137–48; dollar diplomacy of, 61–76, 145–48; and world-ordered diplomacy, 44, 60, 86–87, 91–104, 109–11, 115, 117–18; as Kent Professor of Law at Yale, 87–89; and World War I, 85, 87–99, 102–3, 169; in the League of Nations debate, 89, 99, 154–69; as chief justice of the Supreme Court, 115–17. Books by: *Popular Government,* 87; *The President and His Powers,* 88–89

Taft-Katsura agreement, 47–49; text of, 126–27

Teller Amendment, 40, 43

treaties, U.S. Constitution and, 88–89, 94, 102

U

Unitarianism, 5–6

V

Versailles, Treaty of, 102–4, 109–11, 156–57, 161–62, 165

W

Washington Convention (1907), 66–67

White, Edward D., 116

Wilson, Henry Lane, 71–72

Wilson, Woodrow, 85, 86; Henry Cabot Lodge and, 106–7; Theodore Roosevelt and, 108; William Howard Taft and, 92, 101, 103–4

Woolsey, Theodore Dwight, 7–9, 101

World Court Congress (1915), 92–93

world order, 87, 90, 95, 105, 115

world-ordered diplomacy, 89; Taft and, 44, 60, 86–87, 91–104, 109–11, 117–18

World War I: approach of, 59, 64; immediate impact of, 90, 108; repercussions of, 20; Taft and, 89, 97–98, 102–3

Y

Yale University, 6–8, 11, 87

Z

Zelaya, José, 66